Stories of Slavery
in NEW JERSEY

Stories of Slavery
in NEW JERSEY

RICK GEFFKEN

Foreword from Dr. Walter D. Greason, PhD

THE
Hiſtory
PRESS

Published by The History Press
Charleston, SC
www.historypress.com

Front, left: Unknown young Black woman. *Monmouth County Historical Association.*
Front, right: Charles Reeves. *Mae Smack Edwards.*
Back, top: Peter Still. *Public domain.*
Back, bottom: The Washington family. *National Gallery of Art.*

First published 2021

Manufactured in the United States

ISBN 9781467146678

Library of Congress Control Number: 2020944152

This book is dedicated to the woman of color who enlightened and inspired me:
My friend, the late Mae Smack Edwards

CONTENTS

FOREWORD

For a century, historians have told the history of American slavery from the perspectives of the slaveholders. The temptation was overwhelming because the project of professional history itself focused on kings, emperors, popes and, lastly, presidents. The vast majority of humanity had no history, especially not those (from a European perspective) who were indigenous or African. Given those underlying assumptions, how could any history of American slavery begin from the perspectives of the enslaved? It was an unquestionable impossibility for almost a century.

W.E.B. DuBois, Carter G. Woodson and a generation of labor historians laid the foundations for an intellectual challenge to these approaches between 1900 and 1970. Art was the bridge that allowed the possibility of African humanity, and by extension, history. Music transformed a popular consciousness about the value of Black art. Literature enabled radicals to consider the reality of Black creativity. Moment by moment, year after year, Black intellectuals challenged white supremacy, colonialism and segregation to design new patterns for history.

Clement Price, Giles Wright and Larry Greene followed the pioneering work of Marion Thompson Wright to apply these principles to New Jersey's history. Over the last fifty years, their research made it possible for Graham Russell Hodges to craft new knowledge about the enslavement of Africans and their descendants in the Garden State. His frame described the "rural North" as a paradigm beyond the familiar terrain of the "urban North" and "rural South." A much more detailed portrait of New Jersey's evolution has emerged over the past two decades.

Rick Geffken synthesizes a broad range of historical resources to reconstruct the processes of enslavement in the seventeenth, eighteenth and nineteenth centuries in a variety of small communities in New Jersey. His analysis emerges from a decade of digital resources that were not easily available before the expansion of online collections. Conversations on listserves, websites like Garden State History and collections of editorials about sites like Lewis Morris's Tinton Falls Mill all contribute to the rich tapestry presented here. The result? A detailed examination of slavery as it evolved in places that show that tobacco, cotton and sugar were not the only systems that dehumanized African Americans.

In the context of the new history of capitalism, Geffken provides archivists, librarians and scholars with important new challenges for the decade ahead. The first glimpses of the critical transition to racial enslavement between 1670 and 1760 are apparent in these chapters. Religious institutions and the formative marketplaces reveal the depths of owners', traders' and buyers' respective commitments to an expanding slave trade. This book provides additional resources to understand how the enslavement of Africans shaped the American experiment in ways that reinforce the lessons of the *New York Times Magazine*'s Pulitzer Prize–winning 1619 Project. Academic and popular audiences must consider fundamental revisions in the story of New Jersey because this work provides new clues about the state's early development.

—Dr. Walter D. Greason, PhD
Dean Emeritus, the Honors School, Monmouth University

ACKNOWLEDGEMENTS

Without the generous spirit of the contemporary African American families I've come to know, this book would not have been possible. They shared with me their private and often painful memories, photos and documents. I am grateful to Edwin Edwards, Claire Garland, Jackie Morgan-Stackhouse, Dee Dee Roberts, Gilda Rogers, Inice Shomo Hennessy, Rob Shomo, John Smack, Lorraine Stone and Jean Thomas.

Colgate University's Graham Russell Hodges deserves my special thanks. His pioneering work about slavery in Monmouth County and his subsequent books about the African American experience in New Jersey are always informative and inspirational.

I acknowledge the historians, librarians, researchers and archivists who led me to sources I might otherwise have missed. These include Julius Adekunle, Michael Adelberg, Betty Anderson, Robert Lowe Barnett, Ned Benton, Joe Bilby, Arnold Brown, Don Burden, Jim Davidson, Randall Gabrielan, Pati Githens, Connie Goddard, Joe Grabas, Walter Greason, Joe Hammond, Christine Hanlon, Dana Howell, Mary Hussey, Bob Kelly Jr., Mary Ellyn Kunz, Mary Letson, Evelyn McDowell, Diedre and Tabitha McIntosh, Claudia Ocello, Steve Peter, Judy-Lynne Peters, Steve Ross, Marilyn Rubin, Gary Saretzky, Pat Sherwen, Sam Stephens, Alice Stevenson, Diana Stevenson, Mark Stewart, Rich Veit, Beverly Yackel and Joe Zemla.

Thank you to the many African American researchers and scholars who have written and told their stories as only they can.

A special thanks to my friend George Severini for his assistance in rendering the illustrations in this book to the high quality that readers will enjoy.

INTRODUCTION

Think of the slave, in your hours of glee,
Ye who are treading life's flowery way;
Naught but its rankling thorns has he,
Naught but the gloom of its wintry day.

Think of the slave, in your hours of woe!
What are your sorrows, to that he bears?
Quenching the light of his bosom's glow,
With a life-long stain of gushing tears.

Think of the slave, in your hours of prayer,
When worldly thoughts in your heart are dim;
Offer your thanks for the bliss ye share,
But pray for a brighter lot for him.
—E.M. Chandler

When the Quaker poet Elizabeth Margaret Chandler wrote these verses in the 1830s, she was hopeful that other white Americans would heed her admonitions. Cautiously optimistic, she also wrote, "Terrible in crime and magnitude as the slavery of our country is, I do not despair; apathy must, will awaken, and opposition die; the cause of justice must triumph, or our country must be ruined."

This is a book of stories about Black people enslaved by white people in New Jersey. If that's a hard statement to read, it was equally difficult for me to discover this truth so late in my life. Living in the Garden State for over seven decades now, I'm incredulous that I knew nothing about slavery for most of them. I don't think the good Sisters of St. Francis, nor the Jesuits—teachers who bookended my formal education—were hiding any of this awful history. I want to believe they didn't know about it either.

Slavery was "baked into" New Jersey from its very beginnings. In the 1664–65 *Concession and Agreement of the Lords Proprietors of the Province of New Caesarea, or New Jersey,* Lord John Berkeley and Sir George Carteret granted prospective colonists seventy-five acres of land "for every weaker servant, or slave, male or female, exceeding the age of fourteen years, which any one shall send or carry, arriving there." Meant to jumpstart a new agricultural community, this provision of one of New Jersey's founding documents nonetheless made chattel slavery foundational.

Berkeley and Carteret divided their new American province into East and West Jersey. During the ensuing two centuries, slavery played out somewhat differently in each, so I've organized this book into corresponding halves.

Perhaps the first slave law was the one passed by the Elizabeth-Town General Assembly in 1668. Designed to protect white slave owners from losing their human property, its terms were stark: "[If] any man shall willfully or forcibly steal away any mankind [read *slave*], he shall be put to death."

What followed were decades of increasingly restrictive rules and regulations controlling the behavior of people enslaved in New Jersey. As the Black population increased—peaking at over twelve thousand at the turn of the nineteenth century—white slaveholders lived in escalating fear that their slaves would rebel and revenge their oppressive treatment. Sometimes they did.

Laws were passed that sought to control slaves through the application of severe physical penalties—deformities, burnings, hangings—for even minor infractions. Slaves were forbidden to learn how to read and write, to travel without proper papers or passes or to own firearms or real estate. Harsh punishments were not only doled out to offending slaves but often to their owners as well.

New Jersey's slave laws were often about revenue generation and economic growth and less about enlightened moral positions. For instance, a 1714 statute imposed a ten-pound duty on each imported slave. It was designed to bring in more white servants by making it more expensive to bring in slaves—not to discourage slavery. In any event, there were workarounds to avoid the tax; slaves were imported into other colonies and then brought

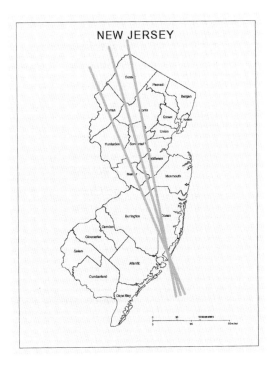

The boundary line between East and West Jersey was never officially settled, with at least three surveys attempted. Shown here are (*left to right*) the Keith (1686), Quintipartite (1676) and Mahacomack (1775) lines. *Robert Lowe Barnett at WestJersey.org, 2020.*

to New Jersey. A few decades later, duties like this were discouraged so that more Black slaves could relieve labor shortages.

Other New Jersey slave laws were actually disincentives. A 1713 change to the slave code addressing the manumission of slaves required a burdensome security deposit of £200 and an additional £20 annually to support the freed person for life. Few slaveholders could afford this payment, which was equivalent to over $50,000 and $5,000 today.

New Jersey grappled with slavery agonizingly slowly. A 1786 law imposed a penalty of fifty pounds for anyone who had brought slaves from Africa after 1776. It called importation a "barbarous custom of bringing the unoffending Africans from their native country." Two years later, it was amended, and strengthened, by adding forfeiture of slave ships and their cargo. But the law didn't abolish slavery. On and on it went for years, depending on labor needs and with little regard for the Black human beings forced to generate profits and to provide easier lives for the white people in charge.

At the national level, there was at least one missed opportunity involving New Jersey. When the newly triumphant United States was forming a government after the Revolutionary War, Thomas Jefferson proposed banning slavery in expansion territories. On April 23, 1784, New Jersey delegate Dr. John Beatty, who agreed with Jefferson, was sick and missed the final vote on the issue. This slavery provision never made it into the Ordinance of 1784.

In 1804, New Jersey passed the Act for the Gradual Abolition of Slavery. This was an attempt to address both the interests of those who depended on enslaved people and their opponents in the growing abolition movement. It mandated that male slaves born after July 4, 1804, had to serve for twenty-five years before manumission and females for twenty years. The act was a compromise, as if there could ever be legal balance to America's original sin. It was a sad admission that some people insisted that their survival depended on human "machines" to grow and harvest their crops, to build their houses, to take care of their children and to perform every demeaning task imaginable.

The New Jersey State Constitution of 1844 declared that "all men are by nature free and independent." As favorable as this sounded to slaves and abolitionists, a year later, the state supreme court ruled that this was only "a general proposition," and it didn't apply to "man in his private, individual or domestic capacity…or to interfere with his domestic relations." In effect, the highest court in New Jersey said that "free and independent" only applied to white men. Once again, New Jersey refused to outlaw slavery.

The 1846 Act to Abolish Slavery, as good as its title sounded, merely changed the description of the subjugated from "slaves" to "apprentices for life." It did, however, allow that children born to slaves thereafter "shall be absolutely free from their birth." How many slaves were affected is difficult to know. Though the next two federal census reports showed decreasing numbers of slaves in New Jersey, the numbers were deceptive because they did not list "apprentices."

Just before the Civil War, the New Jersey census listed eighteen slaves. (The actual number was probably a bit higher.) When the war fought over slavery ended, New Jersey was the last northern state to abolish slavery—reluctantly. Our legislature agreed to ratify the Thirteenth Amendment to the U.S. Constitution in January 1866, only after the required three-fourths of the existing thirty-six states had already done so. New Jersey, which hadn't supported Abraham Lincoln in the elections of 1860 and 1864, shrugged and went along with the fait accompli.

Finally, as if these failures to correct this historic crime against humanity weren't enough, in 1868, New Jersey withdrew its ratification of the Fourteenth Amendment, which granted citizenship and equal protection to all persons born or naturalized in the United States, including former slaves.

In 2007, 140 years after the passage of the Thirteenth Amendment, the New Jersey Legislature passed a resolution expressing "profound regret for the State's role in slavery" and apologized "for the wrong inflicted by slavery and its after effects in the United States of America." This was remarkably late considering that New Jersey was the first state to ratify the Bill of Rights in 1789.

Now, more than a dozen years after the 2007 resolution, discussions of tangible reparations for the injustices of slavery are finally beginning. The Princeton Theological Seminary's 2019 pledge to spend $27 million on scholarships and other programs is a hopeful sign. The state legislature's Black Caucus introduced a bill creating the New Jersey Reparations Task Force, but another long road may loom.

Some of the stories in this book will be familiar; others derive from my original research. The well-known ones are here to help readers understand the context of the more obscure stories. These were real men and women who contributed so much to our state and our country. Acknowledging and understanding our past is necessary for us to change how we live now.

A female acquaintance who helped with my research told me, "I've been called many things in my life—negro, colored, black and now African American." I hope the people in these stories will be recognized for what they were—immense contributors to and inseparable from our New Jersey and American history.

—Rick Geffken, 2020

NOTE: I started writing this book before George Floyd was killed by Minneapolis police on Memorial Day 2020. His death and those of other Black men and women closer to home are the direct results of the shamefully long aftertaste of slavery. I see hope that the resultant national protests will change how we live together everywhere in this country.

Part I.

EAST JERSEY

1

BERGEN COUNTY

THE BEGINNINGS OF SLAVERY IN NEW JERSEY

Well, you talk about trouble, I had it all my days.
Trouble, had it all my days.
Seem like trouble, gonna carry me to my grave.
—Mississippi John Hurt, "Trouble, I've Had It All My Days"

The slave trade in the Americas began when European profiteers brought enslaved Africans to the West Indies in the Caribbean and to South America. Then Atlantic pirates and privateers transported slaves north to the new American colonies.

The Dutch claim to what is New York today was based on Henry Hudson's voyage of discovery in 1609. The Dutch began to develop the trading port of New Amsterdam five years later. Sailing vessels of all kinds found their way to the little outpost on the island that the Lenape natives called Mana-hatta. The curious mix of nationalities in New Amsterdam included Europeans of many nations and Africans from all over the continent, both enslaved and free. The institution of slavery wasn't yet as rigid as it would become. Sometimes owners freed slaves as a reward for faithful service. Black Africans married white Europeans in this time.

The Dutch West India Company (DWI), chartered in 1621, originally eschewed the slave trade, until profits from buying and selling human beings became too large to ignore. The company bought people from Portuguese and Spanish slavers for the burgeoning local markets. New Amsterdam was one stop on the Triangular Trade Route (actually more

NIEUW AMSTERDAM OFTE NUE NIEUW IORX OPT TEYLANT MAN

This watercolor of the trading port of New Amsterdam was done by Johannes Vingboons just before the English took over in 1665. *Gezicht op Nieuw Amsterdam by Johannes Vingboons, 1664.*

of a circular ocean road) as thousands of ships hitchhiked along the North Atlantic Current and the Gulf Stream.

Inevitably, as the Dutch sought to develop more land, slaves were taken across the Noort Rivier (later Hudsons River) to work the bouweries and plantations of farmers on Bergen Neck, in the area the natives called Scheyichbi. To the Dutch, this was part of their colonial province New Netherland. They referred to the land behind a slight geographic rise as Achter Col ("behind the ridge").

In 1629, the DWI began to encourage settlement west of New Amsterdam with enticing offers for men to acquire substantial wealth. Anyone planting a colony of fifty adults within four years was granted sixteen-mile-long swaths of land. These settling patroons, basically feudal chiefs, were required to buy the land from the local Natives.

Michiel Pauw, a burgomaster of Amsterdam, claimed a parcel on a neck of land on the western bank of Hudsons River in July 1630. He called it Pavonia. Pauw later lost his land in a dispute with the company, but subsequent owners were ambitious agriculturalists who needed slaves to till and work their lands. The settlement came to be known as Communipau,

Sketch of the road from Paulus Hook and Hobocken to New Bridge, 1778 John Hills map. *John Hills map, 1778.*

part of modern Jersey City. (Pauw's name means "peacock" in Dutch, which is commemorated today in the mascot of St. Peter's University in Jersey City.)

When a shortage of labor threatened the growth of these new settlements, a convenient solution was near at hand. In exchange for purchasing and developing new lands, the DWI would provide protection and defense and would "import as many blacks as they conveniently could." Thus slavery was established as a bedrock founding principle for Dutch colonists. The DWI had found a way to have its cake and eat it too—at great profit. Not only were imported Blacks important to the development of the territory, but the trade in Africans was in itself highly lucrative. Slaves sold in New Amsterdam yielded many multiples of their purchase price in the islands.

A 1647 document written in Holland verifies how highly valued slaves would be to the Dutch West India Company:

> *Respecting New Netherland: that country is considered to be the most fruitful of all within your High Mightinesses' jurisdiction, and best adapted to raise all sorts of this country produce, such as rye, wheat, barley, peas,*

The founders of Bergen erected a palisade of logs around their settlement on the site of what is now Bergen Square, Jersey City

A 1921 drawing of what the original Bergen Fort in today's Jersey City might have looked like. *History of Hudson County and the Old Village of Bergen, 1921.*

beans, etc., and cattle....We should consider it highly advantageous that a way be opened to allow them [patroons and colonists] *to export their produce even to Brazil...and to trade it off there, and to carry slaves back in return....Slaves being brought and maintained there at a cheap rate, various other descriptions of produce would be raised.*

The tiny village of Bergen dates to 1660, when more and more Dutch settlers farmed the peninsula opposite New Amsterdam. Located on a gently rising ridge to the northwest, and inland of Communipau, the farmers built an eight-hundred-foot-square palisaded fortification at the intersection of several roads to defend themselves against Lenape attacks.

Close to the port of New Amsterdam, with its myriad business opportunities, Bergen produced large quantities of farm products and related goods, which propelled the entire region's growth. Slaves were used as farm laborers, cooks and servants. They were stone and metal craftsmen and manual laborers for the jobs deemed below the status of their owners.

Bergen County became the largest slaveholding county in New Jersey. Census records reveal that only Monmouth County came close to rivalling Bergen in the number of enslaved people recorded in the period between 1790 and the eventual abolishment of slavery in 1865.

JACOB STOFFELSEN WAS THE commissary of stores for the Dutch West India Company in New Amsterdam by 1635. As the overseer of slaves, he once testified before Director Willem Kieft that slaves had built another fort at the southern tip of Manhattan island. Jacob Stoffelsen was also among the earliest Dutch slaveholders in Jersey City.

After Stoffelsen moved across the river, a privateer docking at Harsimus Cove stayed with him as a guest. The ship's captain gave the Dutchman a slave as a gift for his hospitality. Stoffelsen's stepson later took him to court, claiming that he owned half of the slave because he had provided part of a meal for the privateer during his visit. Around 1654, the city court of New Amsterdam upheld Stoffelsen's sole possession of the slave.

GERRIT GERRITSEN LIVED IN Communipau when he began acquiring land in and around Bergen Village. New Amsterdam's governor Peter Stuyvesant appointed him as one of the three *schepen*, or magistrates, of the village. By 1688, two decades after the English took over, the renamed Van Wagenen family (Gerritsen came from Wageningen on the Lower Rhine River in Holland) owned a considerable portion of Bergen, several garden plots outside of the village proper and tracts of farmland on the slope leading toward the Hackensack River. They controlled well over one hundred acres.

Sometime in the early eighteenth century, Gerrit's son Johannis erected a house on the property in Bergen Village. (A subsequent home, still extant in Jersey City, is called the Van Wagenen House.) Van Wagenen slaves tilled the soil, planted and harvested crops and performed the other strenuous tasks required to support a family farm, as did at least five succeeding Gerritsen/ Van Wagenen generations.

The first record of such is the federal census of 1830, in which Hartman Van Wagenen, Gerrit's three-times great-grandson, is noted as the head of a household of ten people attended to by slaves. As with so many of these enslaved Africans, the men and women who literally built New Jersey, we don't know these slaves' names.

DUTCH SLAVE TRADERS BROUGHT Africans to New Amsterdam and East Jersey from Barbados. It would be hard to overstate the impact this small Caribbean island had on American slavery practices. English settlers in Barbados, many of them Quakers, organized their sugar plantations around Black slave labor when they faced a shortage of white indentured servants from England. In effect, Barbadian planters created the template for agricultural slavery in the northern colonies.

After the English takeover of New Netherland in 1664, Barbadians like William Sandford, John Berry and Edmund Kingsland left the island to settle the area between the Passaic and Hackensack Rivers in East Jersey. They called it New Barbadoes and brought their experienced plantation slaves with them. These men knew how to manage slaves to yield the highest farm productivity. As historian Giles Wright has noted, "Because West Indian slaves were familiar with Western customs and work habits, they were highly prized in New Jersey, where master and slaves usually worked and lived in close proximity."

The Schuyler mansion, Fairlawn Manor, was built by slaves with imported stone and bricks in 1719. Expanded over many years, it was demolished in 1924. *Kearny Free Public Library.*

Arent Schuyler bought land on New Barbadoes Neck (Belleville, Kearny, North Arlington and Lyndhurst) from Kingsland for £330 in 1710. Schuyler slaves built his elegant manor house of stone and brick imported from Holland, but they lived in small, barely adequate dwellings of local stone that they cut themselves.

Slave labor was used to construct the solid Dutch houses that characterize Bergen County well into the eighteenth century. They were made of the local brown sandstone, which was as cheap and abundant as the slaves who cut it. Though they worked to build substantial residences for their masters, these slaves were at the same time deemed untrustworthy and needing constant supervision. The Demarest House in Closter, like others of the period, had a window in the kitchen door, said to be for keeping a watchful eye on the household slaves.

One of Schuyler's slaves plowed up a stone of "a somewhat greenish hue, and of considerable weight." He had discovered copper ore—at least according to the romantic legend. The story strains credibility because after the slave received his freedom as a reward, he allegedly asked "to always live with his master." The Schuyler family became exceedingly wealthy thanks to copper. As many as two hundred slaves "crushed, washed from the bedrock, and barreled" one hundred tons of ore per year at the point of its peak productivity. The Schuylers bought slaves from Angola and the Congo specifically to exploit their expertise in African mining operations.

The enslaved workers transported the ore-loaded barrels across the Meadowlands to ferries across the Hudson to New York and onto ships bound for smelting in Holland. It was backbreaking and unhealthy work for these Schuyler slaves. Besides breathing in dust and debris from their labors, their hearing and sight suffered as well.

In partnership with other merchants and prominent businessmen, the Schuyler family imported slaves directly from Africa into Perth Amboy, New Jersey, on their own ships such as the *Catherine*. Of the hundreds of slaves they imported, some were destined for the family's mining efforts, while others were sold for a handsome return on investment. Landing them in Perth Amboy had the added advantage of helping the Schuylers avoid import duties at the port of New York.

No one knows how many slaves died of mining accidents or from the debilitating aftereffects of this brutal work. Arent Schuyler was a founding member of the Second River Dutch Reformed Church (Belleville). A

Arent Schuyler's land on Barbadoes Neck was between the Passaic and Hackensack Rivers. Baren Neck on the map consists of today's Bayonne and Jersey City. *Bayonne Historical Society.*

legend has it that the lime-covered skeletons of some of his miners were found buried in the church basement. The Dutch Reformed Church itself had no official revulsion toward slavery in the colonies. Some of its clergy were slave owners.

Arent Schuyler's son, John, who oversaw the family's mining operations during its most successful years, used his slaves to construct a three-mile-long corduroy road of logs and bridges from the mines to the Hackensack River (the road that became the Belleville Turnpike). Slaves surely also constructed John Schuyler's private game reserve, which Benjamin Franklin noted, enviously, was "a Deer Park, 5 miles round, fenc'd with Cedar Logs, 5 Logs High."

John Schuyler was ultimately indifferent whence his slaves came. During the 1740s and 1750s, his ships brought them to New Jersey and New York from the Caribbean, Africa and even from other American colonies.

(A Schuyler cousin, Elizabeth, married Alexander Hamilton, who was killed in a duel with Aaron Burr in 1804 on the heights of Weehawken, within sight of the Schuyler family mines. Founding father Hamilton had, at best, his own ambiguous feelings about slavery.)

———— ⚬ ————

CONSTABLE POINT, AT THE southern end of Bergen Neck, was another early Dutch settlement along the Hudson River. In August 1757, the *New York Post Boy* ran this ad: "TO BE SOLD. At Van Buskirk's on Kill Van Kull, a parcel of likely Negro Slaves, Men, Women, Boys and Girls, just arrived from Guinea (Africa) in the Sloop 'Williams,' David Griffiths, Commander. Apply to Rice Williams or to said David Griffiths."

A half century before the ad appeared, Pieter Van Buskirk had built his stone farmhouse on a bluff overlooking the shores of New York Bay, at the entrance to the Kill Van Kull (Dutch for "channel from the ridge"). Staten Island is just across the narrow kill. The Van Buskirk estate at Constable Point (today's Bayonne) was an ideal and convenient spot for ships to anchor and offload cargoes of Africans.

A shed adjoining the Van Buskirk house was a holding pen—a jail really—for those slaves awaiting sale. Pieter's son Johannes Van Buskirk apparently kept a dozen or more slaves to work on the family farm, so it's probable that succeeding generations of Van Buskirks were slaveholders too.

Peter Van Buskirk's early eighteenth-century stone house sat on a bluff overlooking New York Bay at the entrance to the Kill Van Kull in what became Bayonne, New Jersey. First History of Bayonne, New Jersey, *1904.*

TWENTY YEARS BEFORE THE Revolutionary War, Thomas Brown, of Dutch and English heritage, owned a four-hundred-acre estate in the Pamrapaugh section of Bergen County (today's Greenville section of Jersey City). A former privateer captain, Brown built his fortunes as a slave trader in the West Indies.

Captain Brown also operated a Hackensack River ferry, further enriching him as he connected the markets of New York and Philadelphia. The profits he made from trading in human beings enabled Brown to build a grander home after a fire destroyed his first. The opulent Retirement Hall, furnished with imported English and French furnishings, not only served as his family's residence, but the basement also held hundreds of slaves over the years. An early twentieth-century report alleges that the basement walls of the old house were imbedded with the chains, manacles, rings and staples used to restrain slaves.

Brown was a member of the Bergen County Standing Committee of Correspondence during the run-up to the Revolution. He is another example of a Patriot who espoused independence from Britain while simultaneously denying the same to the enslaved people who made his own life so comfortable.

RETIREMENT HALL.

Captain Thomas Brown called his home Retirement Hall. It was his residence and a holding pen for hundreds of slaves he sold. *Jersey City Free Public Library.*

Not long after the war, British Loyalists relocating to Canada filed claims for confiscation of "stolen properties"—their appropriated real estate as well as seized slaves. Abraham Van Buskirk (a physician originally from Hackensack who was commissioned as a lieutenant colonel in the British New Jersey Volunteers) said that rebels stole his twenty-year-old "negroe" miller, Sam; his carpenter, Primus, nineteen; Caesar and Quashee; and two others, unnamed.

An 1833 bill of sale for $200 from John J. Van Buskirk to Henry Brinkerhoff stated that Van Buskirk (possibly Abraham's son) "granted sold and released and by these presents do fully clearly and absolutely grant Bargain sell and Release….A Certain Negro man Named Jack, he was Born the Fifteenth Day of April in the year 1794 Aged about thirty nine years…and…will warrant and forever defend the sale of the said Negro man by these presents."

Jack's skill as a carpenter was both his blessing and, obviously, his curse.

THE HORRORS OF PRE-REVOLUTIONARY slavery in Bergen County, and elsewhere in New Jersey, include what can only be described as medieval torture, including burning disobedient slaves at the stake. Shocking as this is to modern sensibilities, eighteenth-century colonists believed that enslaved Africans and their descendants were subhuman and needed to witness extreme punishment for transgressions in order to be controlled.

In 1713, the New Jersey General Assembly passed a law proscribing the eye-for-an-eye Old Testament retribution for crimes committed by people in bondage:

> *All and every Negro, Indian or other Slave who shall murder or otherwise kill...or conspire or attempt the Death of any of Her Majestie's Liege People, not being slaves, or shall commit any Rape...or shall willfully burn any Dwelling House, Barn, Stable, Outhouse, Stack or Stacks of Corn or Hay, or shall willfully Mutilate, Maim or Dismember any of said subjects, not being Slaves...or shall willfully Murder any Negro, Indian or Mulatto Slave within this Province, and thereof be convicted...he, she or they so offending shall suffer the Pains of Death in such Manner as the Aggravation or Enormity of their Crimes...shall merit and require.*

Although this law did not specifically endorse execution by burning, the phrase "such manner" allowed sufficient ambiguity that slaves could be, and were, burned alive in Bergen County. The first of four recorded burnings occurred during the summer of 1735, when Peter Kipp testified against his slave Jack. Kipp told a quickly convened court that "he gave said negro a blow which the said negro resisted and fought with his master, striking him several blows." Jack allegedly scared Kipp away with an ax and yelled that he'd kill him and his son. When Kipp returned with a posse and tied Jack up, the enraged slave said he'd burn his master's house down while he was sleeping.

Though it appeared to be self-defense, Jack's threatening temerity was enough evidence for the court's justices to pronounce the harshest sentence. They ordered the high sheriff of Bergen County to take Jack "to be burnt until he is dead at some convenient place on the road between the Court House and Quacksack." The fight between Jack and Kipp happened on Wednesday, August 13. He was tried on Friday, August 15, and executed by fire the next day.

The three other Black Bergen County men burned for various crimes were two anonymous slaves accused of burning a barn in 1741 at Yellow Point

(Bogota) and Harry, who confessed to killing a white man in Hackensack in 1767. Writing about these recorded atrocities in 1905 with sensationalized detail, William Linn finished his article with this astonishing thought: "It must not be concluded from these lurid pictures that the slaves of New Jersey were cruelly treated as a rule." Linn was wrong; these extraordinarily cruel punishments were indeed the rule—the rule of law.

THE PRECARIOUS LIVES OF enslaved people in Bergen County did not improve much after the American War for Independence, as evidenced by this letter from Isaac Van Gesen of Secaucus in May 1784:

> *Dear Brother, I understand by your accounts that you like the country very much and that you have seen my negro France and that you can with a Bill of Sale from me get him and dispose of him, which I trust that you will sell him to the best advantage….If you hear anything of Daniel Smiths negro Jack I desire that you will send word by your next letter and let know if you can with an order from him sell his negro.*

> *P.S. I will satisfy you for your trouble and defend to you the property of the said Negro. What money you get for him you can dispose of at your pleasure only give me an order.*

A Frenchman traveling through New Jersey a few years after the Revolutionary War correctly observed how justice was unequally distributed when he wrote, "The crime falls on the head of the master; and the slave is thus degraded and punished for the vice of the master….If, as is easy to prove, the crimes of slaves are almost universally the fruit of their slavery, and are in proportion to the severity of their treatment, is it not absurd to recompense the master for his tyranny?"

TWENTIETH-CENTURY HISTORIES OF BERGEN and Hudson County (which separated from Bergen in 1840) are replete with stories of how New Jersey slaves chose to remain living with and serving their former owners after the

Civil War. Supposing some kind of familial devotion, typical of these "feel good" yarns, is the following from Daniel Van Winkle in 1924:

> *After the emancipation of the slaves, so greatly attached had they become to their masters, that many of them absolutely refused to accept their freedom in the sense of self-dependence, always regarding themselves as part and parcel of the old home, from which they did not want to leave. Some of them, addicted to the roving, careless life that seems to have been transmitted to them from far-off ancestors, roamed through the woods and swamps in the vicinity searching for huckleberries, blackberries, or the "snapping" turtle… frost fish or "killies"…mushrooms. The appearance of the "Rovers" with a full supply at the "back kitchen" door was hailed with delight.*

These romanticized, Uncle Remus–like tales are absurd and complete misunderstandings of the motivations and survival skills of newly freed African Americans. No doubt some Black freemen and women might have remained with their former enslavers for a time. Where else would they go? They had little, if any, money or the resources necessary for independent living, renting or buying homes or even moving to a new locale. They were rightfully wary of other strange white people in different towns. They'd most likely be inclined to seek a new life gradually, waiting to hear from other formerly enslaved kin and friends about safer places to dwell where they might support their families.

It is also sadly comical that these manumitted folks are described as having had a "careless life." For generations, African Americans in New Jersey knew all too well how they were cared for—brutally.

As to the skills of food gathering attributed to their African ancestry, the very phrase Van Winkle uses, "transmitted to them from far-off ancestors," is demeaning. He writes as if these newly freed people were merely unsophisticated savages who did not have or were unable to develop their own skills. In fact, generations of enslaved people had supplemented their meager slave-owner-provided diets by foraging and planting what they could on small plots of land, sometimes surreptitiously. Once freed, they were not cavorting through any woods on jaunts in blissful communion with nature. They were finding and consuming needed calories wherever they could to feed themselves and their loved ones.

Van Winkle claimed that white people "hailed with delight" at former slaves calling on them. This stretches credulity. Magically, white slave owners and others who had witnessed and approved the centuries-old subjugation and oppression of Black people suddenly found these freed folks amusing food vendors? Only if you believe Van Winkle as he writes about "the sonorous and melodious voice of 'Old Yon' as he cried 'fresh buttermilk.'" Or that "'Old Betty's' chicken and eggs possessed a peculiarly appetizing flavor, and her culinary accomplishments were especially appreciated by the younger generation when carried by their wanderings beyond the dinner hour at home." Would that we had Yon's or Betty's versions of how they were actually treated, and paid, at the back-kitchen doors they knocked on.

A more egregious example of history rewritten—actually *unwritten*, because of what it ignored—is a 1921 publication by the Trust Company of Jersey City, titled *History of Hudson County and the Old Village of Bergen*. There is not a single mention of the slaves (nor slavery, nor Africans) who contributed immensely to the growth of a city with a significant African American community today. (Author's note: when I was growing up in nearby North Bergen during the 1950s, slavery in New Jersey wasn't taught in schools.)

⸻ ⸻

NEW BARBADOES PROSPERED THROUGH the forced labor of thousands of African and West Indian slaves. Their immense contributions were unrecognized, unappreciated and taken for granted. The life and dedication of one man speaks to the intense bias that persisted in the Bergen County community for many years.

Samuel Eli Cornish devoted himself to the ministry and education of Black people. He was born free, became an ordained minister and founded the New Demeter Street Presbyterian Church in New York City in 1821. He edited *Freedom's Journal*, the first Black-owned-and-operated newspaper (1827) in the United States. The paper sought to be the counterweight to a white-dominated press. It was abolitionist, argued for Black men's right to vote and against colonization efforts and denounced lynchings. Cornish subsequently wrote for other newspapers and was a charter member of the New York Anti-Slavery Society, which had both Black and white adherents.

Cornish's concerns for his fellow African Americans focused on their poverty. He understood that the lack of resources available to Black families prevented them from educating their children. The youngsters had no choice but to work to contribute to household income. Cornish realized that simple necessities, like the lack of warm clothing in the winter, was another

35

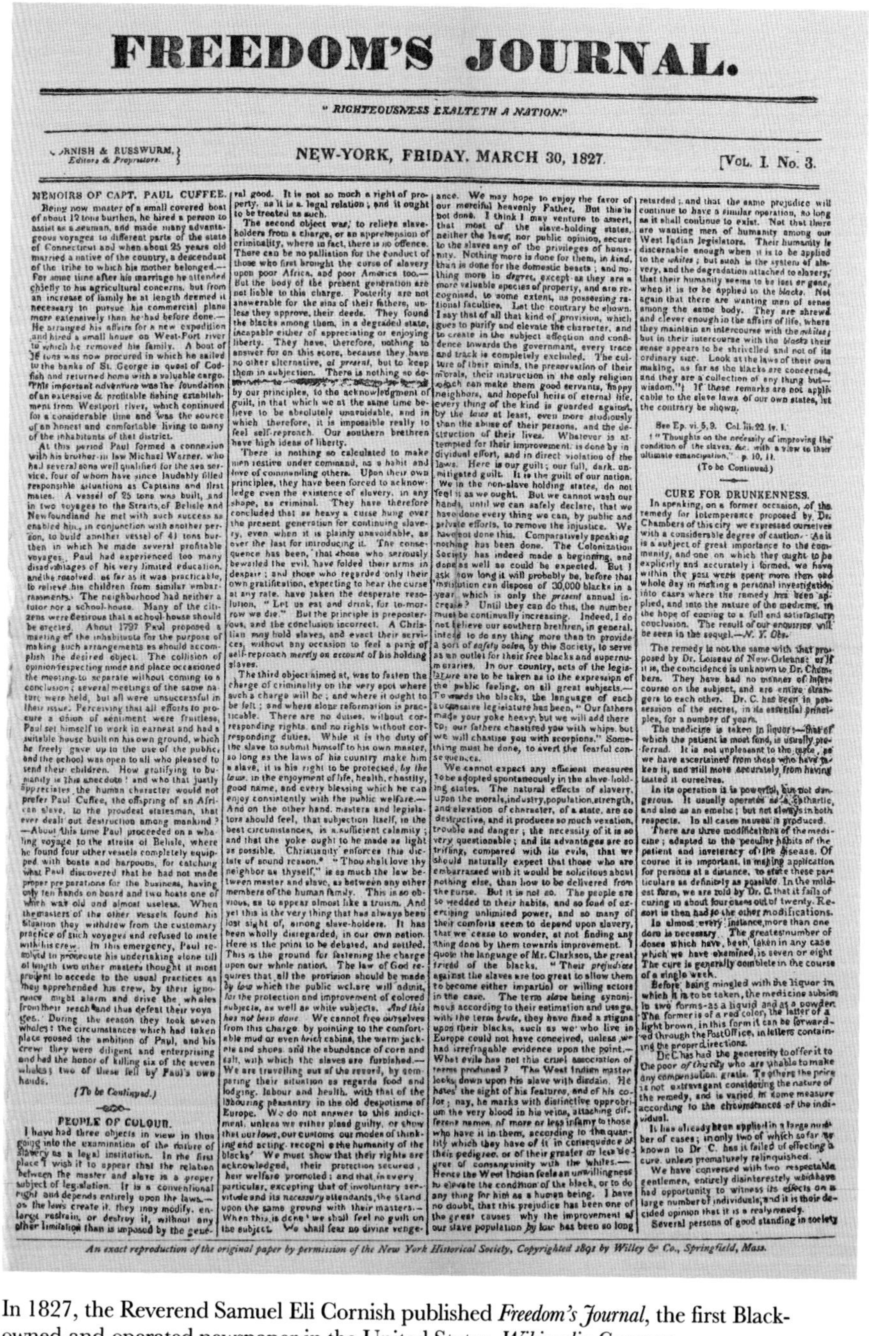

FREEDOM'S JOURNAL.

"RIGHTEOUSNESS EXALTETH A NATION."

CORNISH & RUSSWURM, Editors & Proprietors.

NEW-YORK, FRIDAY, MARCH 30, 1827.

[VOL. I. NO. 3.

MEMOIRS OF CAPT. PAUL CUFFEE.

Being now master of a small covered boat of about 12 tons burthen, he hired a person to assist as a seaman, and made many advantageous voyages to different parts of the state of Connecticut and when about 25 years old married a native of the country, a descendant of the tribe to which his mother belonged.—For some time after his marriage he attended chiefly to his agricultural concerns, but from an increase of family he at length deemed it necessary to pursue his commercial plans more extensively than he had before done.—He arranged his affairs for a new expedition and hired a small house on West-Port river to which he removed his family. A boat of 18 tons was now procured in which he sailed to the banks of St. George in quest of Codfish and returned home with a valuable cargo. This important adventure was the foundation of an extensive & profitable fishing establishment from Westport river, which continued for a considerable time and was the source of an honest and comfortable living to many of the inhabitants of that district.

At this period Paul formed a connexion with his brother-in law Michael Warner, who had several sons well qualified for the sea service, four of whom have since laudably filled responsible situations as Captains and first mates. A vessel of 25 tons was built, and in two voyages to the Straits of Belisle and Newfoundland he met with such success as enabled him, in conjunction with another person, to build another vessel of 41 tons burthen in which he made several profitable voyages. Paul had experienced too many disadvantages of his very limited education, and he resolved, as far as it was practicable, to relieve his children from similar embarrassments. The neighborhood had neither a tutor nor a school-house. Many of the citizens were desirous that a school-house should be erected. About 1797 Paul proposed a meeting of the inhabitants for the purpose of making such arrangements as should accomplish the desired object. The collision of opinion respecting mode and place occasioned the meeting to separate without coming to a conclusion; several meetings of the same nature were held, but all were unsuccessful in their issue. Perceiving that all efforts to procure a union of sentiment were fruitless, Paul set himself to work in earnest and had a suitable house built on his own ground, which he freely gave up to the use of the public, and the school was open to all who pleased to send their children. How gratifying to humanity is this anecdote! and who that justly appreciates the human character would not prefer Paul Cuffee, the offspring of an African slave, to the proudest statesman, that ever dealt out destruction among mankind?—About this time Paul proceeded on a whaling voyage to the straits of Belisle, where he found four other vessels completely equipped with boats and harpoons, for catching what Paul discovered that he had not made proper preparations for the business, having only ten hands on board and two boats one of which was old and almost useless. When the masters of the other vessels found his situation they withdrew from the customary practice of such voyages and refused to mate with his crew. In this emergency, Paul resolved to prosecute his undertaking alone till at length two other masters thought it most prudent to accede to the usual practices as they apprehended his crew, by their ignorance might alarm and drive the whales from their reach and thus defeat their voyages. During the season they took seven whales: the circumstances which had taken place roused the ambition of Paul, and his crew: they were diligent and enterprising and had the honor of killing six of the seven whales; two of these fell by Paul's own hands.

(To be Continued.)

PEOPLE OF COLOUR.

I have had three objects in view in thus going into the examination of the nature of slavery as a legal institution. In the first place I wish it to appear that the relation between the master and slave is a proper subject of legislation. It is a conventional right and depends entirely upon the laws.—as the laws create it, they may modify, enlarge, restrain, or destroy it, without any other limitation than is imposed by the general good. It is not so much a right of property, as it is a legal relation; and it ought to be treated as such.

The second object was, to relieve slave-holders from a charge, or an apprehension of criminality, where in fact, there is no offence. There can be no palliation for the conduct of those who first brought the curse of slavery upon poor Africa, and poor America too.—But the body of the present generation are not liable to this charge. Posterity are not answerable for the sins of their fathers, unless they approve their deeds. They found the blacks among them, in a degraded state, incapable either of appreciating or enjoying liberty. They have, therefore, nothing to answer for on this score, because they have no other alternative, *at present*, but to keep them in subjection. There is nothing so de- [illegible] by our principles, to the acknowledgment of guilt, in that which we at the same time believe to be absolutely unavoidable, and in which therefore, it is impossible really to feel self-reproach. Our southern brethren have high ideas of liberty.

There is nothing so calculated to make men restive under command, as a habit and love of commanding others. Upon their own principles, they have been forced to acknowledge even the existence of slavery, in any shape, as criminal. They have therefore concluded that as heavy a curse hung over the present generation for continuing slavery, even when it is plainly unavoidable, as over the last for introducing it. The consequence has been, that those who seriously bewailed the evil, have folded their arms in despair; and those who regarded only their own gratification, expecting to hear the curse at any rate, have taken the desperate resolution, "Let us eat and drink, for to-morrow we die." But the principle is preposterous, and the conclusion incorrect. A Christian *may* hold slaves, and exact their services, without any occasion to feel a pang of self-reproach *merely on account* of his holding slaves.

The third object aimed at, was to fasten the charge of criminality on the *very* spot where such a charge will be; and where it ought to be felt; and where alone reformation is practicable. There are no duties, without corresponding rights, and no rights without corresponding duties. While it is the duty of the slave to submit himself to his own master, so long as the laws of his country make him a slave, it is his right to be protected, *by the laws*, in the enjoyment of life, health, chastity, good name, and every blessing which he can enjoy consistently with the public welfare.—And on the other hand, masters and legislators should feel, that subjection itself, in the best circumstances, is a sufficient calamity; and that the yoke ought to be made as light as possible. Christianity enforces this dictate of sound reason.* "Thou shalt love thy neighbor as thyself," is as much the law between master and slave, as between any other members of the human family. This is so obvious, as to appear almost like a truism. And yet this is the very thing that has always been lost sight of, among slave-holders. It has been wholly disregarded, in our own nation. Here is the point to be debated, and settled. This is the ground for fastening the charge upon our whole nation. The law of God requires that all the provision should be made *by law* which the public welfare will admit, *for* the protection and improvement of colored subjects, as well as white subjects. *And this has not been done.* We cannot free ourselves from this charge, by pointing to the comfortable mud or even *brick* cabins, the warm jackets and shoes, and the abundance of corn and salt, with which the slaves are furnished.—We are travelling out of the record, by comparing their situation as regards food and lodging, labour and health, with that of the labouring peasantry in the old despotisms of Europe. We do not answer to this indictment, unless we either plead guilty, or show that our *laws*, our customs, our modes of thinking and acting, recognize the humanity of the blacks. We must show that their rights are acknowledged, their protection secured, their welfare promoted; and that, in every particular, excepting that of involuntary servitude and its *necessary* attendants, they stand upon the same ground with their masters.—When this is done, we shall feel no guilt on the subject. We shall fear no divine vengeance. We may hope to enjoy the favor of our merciful heavenly Father. But this is not done. I think I may venture to assert, that most of the slave-holding states, neither the laws, nor public opinion, secure to the slaves any of the privileges of humanity. Nothing more is done for them, in *kind*, than is done for the domestic beasts; and nothing more in *degree*, except as they are a more valuable species of property, and are recognised, to some extent, as possessing rational faculties. Let the contrary be shown. I say that of all that kind of provision, which goes to purify and elevate the character, and to create in the subject affection and confidence towards the government, every trace and track is completely excluded. The culture of their minds, the preservation of their morals, their instruction in the only religion which can make them good servants, happy neighbors, and hopeful heirs of eternal life, every thing of the kind is guarded against, by the *laws* at least, even more studiously than the abuse of their persons, and the destruction of their lives. Whatever is attempted for their improvement, is done by individual effort, and in direct violation of the laws. Here is our guilt; our full, dark, unmitigated guilt. It is the guilt of our nation. We in the non-slave holding states, do not feel it as we ought. But we cannot wash our hands, until we can safely declare, that we have done every thing we can, by public and private efforts, to remove the injustice. We have not done this. Comparatively speaking nothing has been done. The Colonization Society has indeed made a beginning, and done as well as could be expected. But I ask how long it will probably be, before that institution can dispose of 30,000 blacks in a year which is only the *present* annual increase? Until they can do this, the number must be continually increasing. Indeed, I do not believe our southern brethren, in general, intend to do any thing more than to provide a sort of *safety valve*, by this Society, to serve as an outlet for their free blacks and supernumeraries. In our country, acts of the legislature are to be taken as to the expression of the public feeling, on all great subjects.—Towards the blacks, the language of each successive legislature has been, "Our fathers made your yoke heavy, but we will add thereto; our fathers chastised you with whips, but we will chastise you with scorpions." Something must be done, to avert the fearful consequences.

We cannot expect any efficient measures to be adopted spontaneously in the slave-holding states. The natural effects of slavery, upon the morals, industry, population, strength, and elevation of character, of a state, are so destructive, and it produces so much vexation, trouble and danger; the necessity of it is so very questionable; and its advantages are so trifling, compared with its evils, that we should naturally expect that those who are embarrassed with it would be solicitous about nothing else, than how to be delivered from the curse. But it is not so. The people are so wedded to their habits, and so fond of exercising unlimited power, and so many of their comforts seem to depend upon slavery, that we cease to wonder, at not finding any thing done by them towards improvement. I quote the language of Mr. Clarkson, the great friend of the blacks. "Their *prejudices* against the slaves are too great to allow them to become either impartial or willing actors in the case. The term *slave* being synonimous according to their estimation and usage, with the term *brute*, they have fixed a stigma upon their blacks, such as we who live in Europe could not have conceived, unless we had irrefragable evidence upon the point.—What evils has not this cruel association of terms produced? The West Indian master looks down upon his slave with disdain. He hates the sight of his features, and of his color; nay, he marks with distinctive opprobrium the very blood in his veins, attaching different names, of more or less infamy to those who have it in them, according to the quantity which they have of it in consequence of their pedigree, or of their greater or less degree of consanguinity with the whites.—Hence the West Indian feels an unwillingness to elevate the condition of the black, or to do any thing for him as a human being. I have no doubt, that this prejudice has been one of the great causes why the improvement of our slave population *by law* has been so long retarded; and that the same prejudice will continue to have a similar operation, so long as it shall continue to exist. Not that there are wanting men of humanity among our West Indian legislators. Their humanity is discernable enough when it is to be applied to the *whites*; but such is the system of slavery, and the degradation attached to slavery, that their humanity seems to be lost or gone, when it is to be applied to the *blacks*. Not again that there are wanting men of sense among the same body. They are shrewd and clever enough in the affairs of life, where they maintain an intercourse with the *whites*; but in their intercourse with the *blacks* their sense appears to be shrivelled and not of its ordinary size. Look at the laws of their own making, as far as the blacks are concerned, and they are a collection of any thing but—wisdom."† If these remarks are not applicable to the slave laws of our own states, let the contrary be shown.

* See Ep. vi. 5, 9. Col. iii. 22. iv. 1.

† "Thoughts on the necessity of improving the condition of the slaves, &c. with a view to their ultimate emancipation," p. 10, 11.

(To be Continued.)

CURE FOR DRUNKENNESS.

In speaking, on a former occasion, of the remedy for intemperance proposed by Dr. Chambers of this city we expressed ourselves with a considerable degree of caution. As it is a subject of great importance to the community, and one on which they ought to be explicitly and accurately informed, we have within the past week spent more than one whole day in making a personal investigation into cases where the remedy has been applied, and into the nature of the medicine, in the hope of coming to a full and satisfactory conclusion. The result of our enquiries will be seen in the sequel.—*N. Y. Obs.*

The remedy is not the same with that proposed by Dr. Loiseau of New-Orleans; or if it is, the coincidence is unknown to Dr. Chambers. They have had no manner of intercourse on the subject, and are entire strangers to each other. Dr. C. has been in possession of the secret, in its essential principles, for a number of years.

The medicine is taken in liquor:—that of which the patient is most fond, is usually preferred. It is not unpleasant to the taste, as we have ascertained from those who have taken it, and still more accurately, from having tasted it ourselves.

In its operation it is powerful, but not dangerous. It usually operates as a cathartic, and also as an emetic; but not always in both respects. In all cases nausea is produced.

There are three modifications of the medicine; adapted to the peculiar habits of the patient and inveteracy of the disease. Of course it is important, in making application for persons at a distance, to state these particulars as definitely as possible. In the mildest form, we are told by Dr. C. that it fails of curing in about four cases out of twenty. Resort is then had to the other modifications.

In almost every instance, more than one dose is necessary. The greatest number of doses which have been taken in any case which we have examined, is seven or eight. The cure is generally complete in the course of a single week.

Before being mingled with the liquor in which it is to be taken, the medicine subsists in two forms—as a liquid and as a powder. The former is of a red color, the latter of a light brown, in this form it can be forwarded through the Post Office, in letters containing the proper directions.

Dr. C. has had the generosity to offer it to the poor *of the city* who are unable to make any compensation, gratis. To others the price is not extravagant considering the nature of the remedy, and is varied in some measure according to the circumstances of the individual.

It has already been applied in a large number of cases; in only two of which so far as known to Dr. C. has it failed of effecting a cure, unless prematurely relinquished.

We have conversed with two respectable gentlemen, entirely disinterested, who have had opportunity to witness its effects on a large number of individuals, and it is their decided opinion that it is a real remedy.

Several persons of good standing in society

An exact reproduction of the original paper by permission of the New York Historical Society, Copyrighted 1891 by Willey & Co., Springfield, Mass.

In 1827, the Reverend Samuel Eli Cornish published *Freedom's Journal*, the first Black-owned-and-operated newspaper in the United States. *Wikimedia Commons.*

REV.ᵈ SAMUEL CORNISH

Samuel Eli Cornish moved from New York City to New Barbadoes Neck (Belleville) as a free Black man, but he did not escape the bias and prejudice of the era. *New York Public Library.*

Reverend Theodore Wright was the first Black man to attend Princeton Theological Seminary. *Wikimedia Commons.*

impediment keeping children away from school. He formed organizations specifically to remedy these basic issues.

The Reverend Cornish moved to New Barbadoes (Belleville) a century and a quarter after it was settled by slaveholders. Despite his decades-long religious and civic endeavors, he found the prejudice of the white establishment unbearable, so he relocated to Newark. Chastened but undaunted, he began again, this time as pastor of the Plane Street Colored Presbyterian Church. Cornish knew that the church was nearly destroyed in a riot after an abolition meeting several years earlier, but he was nothing if not resolute.

Reverend Cornish was strongly opposed to the aims of the American Colonization Society (ACS), which encouraged the "repatriation" of free American Blacks to Africa. In an 1840 open letter to the prominent white politicians Theodore Frelinghuysen (the seventh president of Rutgers University) and Benjamin Butler (a Massachusetts attorney), who supported the society, Cornish and his colleague, the Reverend Theodore Wright (the first African American to attend Princeton Theological Seminary), refuted the assertion that "the free colored people have hearts which yearn for Africa." After a reasoned point-by-point argument showing the absurdity of the claim of Christian motives for repatriation, the men's letter identified the true economic and political basis of this attempt to export American citizens: "This prejudice, springing out of slavery, has been kept up by the cooperation of influential men at the North with Southern slaveholders."

The idea of moving American Blacks to Africa had surprising support from the most

THE

COLONIZATION SCHEME CONSIDERED,

IN

ITS REJECTION BY THE COLORED PEOPLE—IN ITS

TENDENCY TO UPHOLD CASTE—IN ITS

UNFITNESS FOR CHRISTIANIZING AND CIVILIZING

THE ABORIGINES OF AFRICA,

AND FOR PUTTING A STOP TO

THE AFRICAN SLAVE TRADE:

IN A LETTER TO

THE HON. THEODORE FRELINGHUYSEN

AND

THE HON. BENJAMIN F. BUTLER;

BY

SAMUEL E. CORNISH AND THEODORE S. WRIGHT,

PASTORS OF THE COLORED PRESBYTERIAN CHURCHES IN THE CITIES OF
NEWARK AND NEW YORK.

NEWARK:
PRINTED BY AARON GUEST, 191 MARKET-STREET.

1840.

Samuel Cornish and his colleague the Reverend Theodore Wright refuted the idea that African Americans wanted to "return" to Africa. They called it a "Colonization Scheme." *African Slave Trade document, Cornish and Wright, 1840.*

famous nineteenth-century American political figure, Abraham Lincoln. His great-great-grandfather Mordecai Lincoln was a blacksmith who had migrated west from New Jersey. Before he was elected to national office and issued the Emancipation Proclamation, Abraham Lincoln was a member of the Illinois Colonization Society. In 1857, Lincoln said, "the separation of the races [to be the] only perfect preventive of amalgamation.... Such separation, if ever effected at all, must be effected by colonization." Lincoln was still considering the merits of relocating slaves until he was assassinated in April 1865.

━━━•━━━

The train jumped track some time ago
You can't root that heavy load
It's all downhill from now
And be sure we paid the toll
The train jumped track some time ago.
—*Cody Jinks, "Heavy Load"*

Bergen/Hudson County played an important role in the Underground Railroad (UGRR), serving as the gateway to New York City, via the Hudson River, and other pathways to freedom in Canada. Jersey City, the very site where slavery was initially introduced to New Jersey by seventeenth-century Dutch farmers, became an important UGRR station during the nineteenth century.

Runaways sought shelter in safehouses for as long as slavery existed. What we think of as the formal UGRR became the primary engine of escape in the years leading up to the Civil War. Canada was seen as a "promised land" after Britain abolished slavery in all of its colonies in 1833. Escaped slaves from the South could flee along the Delaware River in western New Jersey (with its many kindly and accommodating Quakers) and then traverse the narrow portion of New Jersey along the Trenton-Princeton corridor toward the Amboys. From there, it was a short boat ride to Staten Island and then to New York City and beyond. Alternatively, arriving at Jersey City, called the "last station in New Jersey," the escapee could chance the Hudson River to Canada.

The Fugitive Slave Act of 1850 might as well have been the incorporation papers of the UGRR. Besides enabling slaveholders to legally demand return of "a person held to service or labor in any State or Territory of the United States," the law proscribed severe penalties for citizens who assisted escaped slaves. Slave catchers had new urgency to seek financial reward for capturing any Black person, enslaved or free. Runaway slaves and abolitionists reacted with alarm to the law, thus increasing UGRR traffic.

In 1908, a Jersey City newspaperman named Alexander MacLean recalled his family's UGRR station:

> *It is probable that many of these shelters [for runaways] were similar to that provided in my father's barn. This was off the main line, about three miles from Newark. It had a sleeping place in the loft behind the hay,*

supplied with horse blankets, and hay for bedding. When the retreat was in use, a ladder was placed in a sheltered position against the back of the barn, thus offering a means of escape if enemies entered below....The fugitive arrived at the barn sometime during the night, frequently without notice. Food was carried into the loft very early in the morning, and the children on the farm were notified to keep away from the barn during the day. They soon learned when there was "a fresh coon" in the barn and were early impressed with the need for knowing nothing about the presence of these strange visitors. After sleeping most of the day in strict seclusion, the fugitives were forwarded to Jersey City.

Even the language of helpful abolitionist sympathizers like MacLean reflected the bias and prejudice of the times by using denigrating terminology—"a fresh coon"—for the people they were actively assisting.

MacLean described small sloops and schooners picking up runaways at Jersey City's Washington Street docks at Harsimus Cove. The escaped slaves would sometimes hide under barges laden with lumber or coal, bound for New York City or ports farther up the Hudson. In return for free passage, they worked pumping water out of the boats and loading and unloading cargo.

Freedom via the UGRR was never guaranteed because slave catchers knew where to look for their quarry too. Newspaperman MacLean mentions one particularly harrowing escape at Hudson Street: "The guides shook off the pursuers and reached a coal-laden boat discharging a cargo, where the runaway was placed in a small, cave-like compartment beneath the cabin of the boat, the entrance to which was then covered with coal; there, half smothered by coaldust, the fugitive remained in hiding until the pursuit ceased, and he could be dug out and started again on his way to freedom."

As is the case so often in these reports, this individual escaped slave is neither named, nor is there a subsequent report of his eventual fate. Did he reach freedom? Where? How would the escapee himself have described this dramatic episode in his life? Writing less than fifty years after the national abolition of slavery, MacLean says that "how many runaways were carried over the Jersey City and Hoboken ferries is not known." He then immediately contradicts himself: "It is certain that many of the individual operators had passed a thousand fugitives through their care, and that, of something over one hundred thousand slaves who were aided to freedom, more than sixty thousand went through Jersey City."

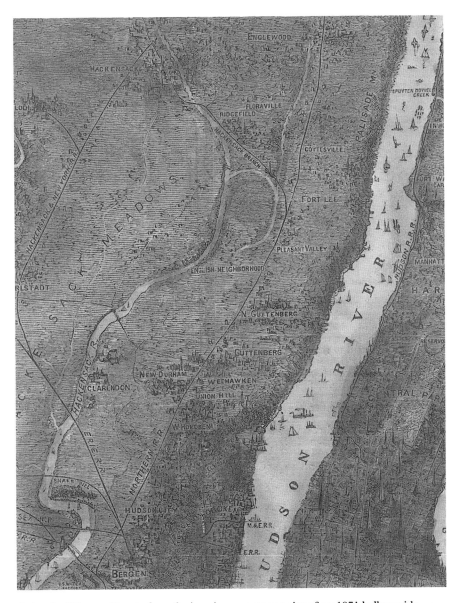

A sketch of Bergen County from the imaginary vantage point of an 1871 balloon ride shows its proximity to New York City on the other side of the Hudson River. Harper's Weekly *magazine, 1871.*

Other prominent Jersey City citizens used their personal homes as safe houses as well. Dr. Henry D. Holt published the *Jersey City Advertiser and Bergen Republican* before he became a physician around 1840. A dedicated abolitionist, Dr. Holt established an Underground Railroad station at his home on Washington Street, near the Hudson River's Morris Canal Basin.

———•———

IT'S IMPOSSIBLE TO KNOW with certainty who were the last slaves freed in Bergen County, although one married couple are good candidates. A farmer named Jacob Van Wagoner of New Barbadoes signed an August 1832 manumission, which freed "my Negro slave Called Tobe of the age of thirty or thereabouts."

Tobe met and married a Hackensack woman named Ice five years later. The pair worked as a team for Henry Brinkerhoff in the English Neighborhood at the Hackensack River before they moved to Fort Lee to work at various domestic jobs, washing clothes, among other tasks. No matter their freedom, they could not escape the hardships of their lives. Tobe drank heavily. He and his wife ended up in the poor house. Tobe died in 1883 and Ice just a few years later. They are buried in the Edgewater Memorial (Vreeland) Cemetery in the family plot of a kindly friend of theirs, John S. Watkins.

2

SLAVERY TAKES HOLD IN MONMOUTH COUNTY

I'm gonna find me another home,
Find it way out in the woods.
—Lightnin' Hopkins, "Home in the Woods"

Although he was not the first man to introduce slavery into the Jerseys, Lewis Morris used slaves in his East Jersey ironworks as early as the 1670s. Dutch traders had forced Africans to work their Bergen County plantations fifty years earlier. However, the sheer scale of Morris's use of chattel slavery was new to the proprietary colony. Morris brought dozens of his Barbadian sugar plantation slaves with him when he moved north to seek new profit opportunities. They toiled on his Tinton Manor estate, located in what he would christen Monmouth County. Both his estate and the county were named for Tintern, Monmouthshire, in Wales, where the Morris family originated.

Lewis Morris and his brother Richard were successful planters who took advantage of the opportunity to expand their fame and fortunes in the English colonies two thousand miles to the north on the Atlantic coast.

After Peter Stuyvesant surrendered Dutch New Amsterdam to Colonel Richard Nicholls in August 1664–65, the English military man renamed the promising seaport New York after his patron, James, Duke of York. In 1668, the Morris brothers partnered on a 520-acre tract in what had once been Jonas Bronck's land east of Harlem Creek. They called the plantation Morrisania. A section of the Bronx retains that designation to this day.

Lewis Morris also owned a house at the southern tip of Manhattan, next door to one of New York's prominent merchants, Cornelius Steenwyck,

The Lewis Morris family crest evoked a battle during the mid-seventeenth-century English Civil Wars. *New York Historical Society.*

who made his money selling tobacco, salt and slaves. The two ambitious men became friends and sought business deals together. By 1672, Steenwyck was on the governing Council of New York, connecting Morris to powerful politicians.

Lewis Morris was not quite ready to abandon living at his West Indian plantation, and returned to Barbados. The deaths of Richard Morris and his wife, Sarah, in 1672 caused Lewis to go back to New York to administer to their estate and, not inconsequentially, to care for their infant son, Lewis, who'd been named for his uncle.

In 1674–75, Lewis Morris joined with Steenwyck to finance an existing bog iron mill in Shrewsbury, East Jersey. The ironworks was owned by James Grover, Richard Hartshorne and John Bowne. The trio needed additional capital to keep the enterprise running, and the two new investors were eager to expand their own influence and fortunes.

Lewis Morris had another reason to leave Barbados for good around this time. A group of slaves were caught conspiring to murder their white masters in 1676. The European planters and Barbados authorities put this plot down brutally—those suspected of taking part were "burned alive, beheaded, and otherwise executed for their horrid crimes." The island government proposed that none of the rebellious negroes could be bought or sold because they were afraid the contagion would spread elsewhere. Perhaps this potential economic loss is what finally spurred Lewis Morris to take his sixty or so slaves north with him. But he had another business incentive too.

Morris eventually took over complete ownership of the ironworks and purchased thousands of additional acres of surrounding land. He was well on his way to becoming the richest man in East Jersey thanks to the mill's production of valuable bar iron, together with his mercantile interests in New York and the sale of his sugar plantations in the Caribbean. Accounting records from the Shrewsbury Iron Works list 1676 expenses for building a "negro house" on the property, which sheltered the first

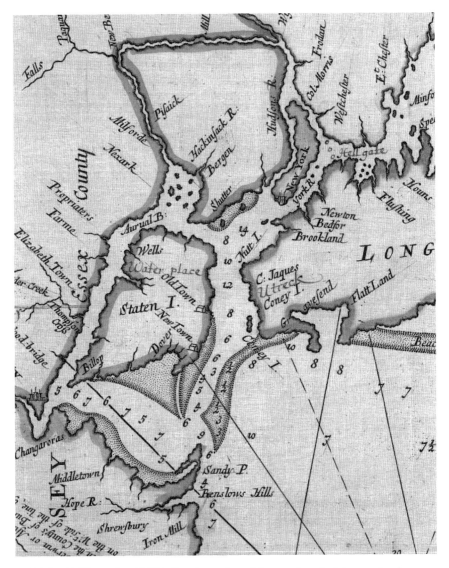

Lewis Morris's Tinton Iron Mill in East Jersey (*lower left*) was only a day's journey by sloop from New York and Morrisania. *"A New Mapp of East and West New Jarsay,"* John Thornton, 1706.

enslaved men brought en masse to East Jersey. It was notably separate from the "white man's house."

A 1679 description of what Morris owned in East Jersey notes, "There is within its jurisdiction Colonel Morice [*sic*], his Mannour, being about six thousand acres, wherein are his iron Mills, his Mannours, and diverse other buildings for his servants and dependents there, together with 60 or 70 negroes, about the Mill and Husbandries, in that plantation."

This iron mill was located on the "Falles Creek," now known as Pine Brook, a tributary of the Swimming River. Well into the twenty-first century, a Tinton Falls neighborhood called Pine Brook is a largely African American community. No contemporary Pine Brook family has self-identified as descendants of Morris slaves, although the connection seems possible.

An interesting, if confounding, aspect of Lewis Morris's early life is that he was a Quaker. Despite our modern perceptions, early Quakers were not abolitionists. Morris became a member of the Society of Friends (the sect's formal name) while he was still in Barbados. He was described as a "severe Quaker." Missionary Friends had visited the island, proselytizing for converts. Perhaps Morris was swayed by their appeal to former soldiers disillusioned by war. He and his brother played active military roles in the

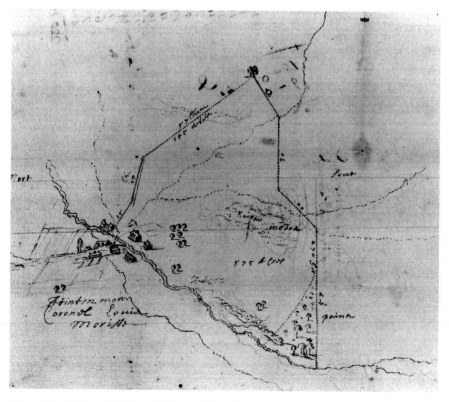

Colonel Lewis Morris's Tinton Manor at Falles Creek (today's Pine Brook) appears on this 1676 surveyor's sketch. *Monmouth County Historical Association.*

mid-century English Civil Wars. The Morris bothers had supported the Parliamentarians, and Lewis had advised Admiral Sir William Penn during naval actions in the Caribbean. Perhaps Lewis Morris had seen enough futility, death and destruction and, impressed by visiting Quakers, embraced their tenets. Lewis Morris's connection to Admiral Penn, whose famous son founded Pennsylvania, would have an interesting subtext regarding one particular slave, as we will see.

At his death in 1690–91, Lewis Morris's Tinton Manor inventory listed sixty-six enslaved men, women and children valued at £844, equivalent to $2.3 million today. The entirety of the plantation was valued at £6,000 (over $16 million now), so the known Morris slaves made up almost 15 percent of his estimated worth in Monmouth County alone. However, a private inventory of slaves made by his nephew, Lewis, indicates that there were actually twice as many slaves. These human beings represented almost a third of the total value of Tinton Manor. The Morris family would not have attained their great wealth without the literal blood, sweat and tears of these enslaved people.

In a 1976 Princeton University doctoral thesis, John Strassburger wrote: "Lewis Morris inherited more slaves than the total number owned by anyone else then living in New York or New Jersey. Even in Virginia, Morris would have qualified as a large slave holder." The sixty-six inventoried enslaved people were nearly 60 percent of all of the slaves in East Jersey in 1691, according to the research of Colgate University scholar Dr. Graham Russell Hodges.

A confounding aspect of the Morris family's relationship to slavery involves the relationship Lewis Morris and his nephew, Lewis, had with George Keith. A Scotch Presbyterian by birth, Keith was an early convert to the Religious Society of Friends. Keith had traveled on missions in Europe with Quaker founder George Fox and William Penn. In 1685, Keith was appointed surveyor-general of the East Jersey Province and was rewarded with a huge tract of Monmouth County land for his efforts.

During this period, Lewis Morris Sr. hired Keith to tutor his nephew. Just two years after the death of Morris Sr., George Keith published *An Exhortation & Caution to Friends Concerning Buying or Keeping of Negroes*, considered an early abolitionist tract. In this searing document, Keith argued for observance of "that Golden Rule and Law, To do to others what we would have others do to us." He advocated setting Negroes free and educating their children.

Keith and the younger Lewis Morris were so close that when Keith converted yet again, this time to Anglicism, the pair began to hold religious services at Tinton Manor. Christ Church in Shrewsbury, New Jersey, considers them to be its founders. Yet despite all that Keith believed and taught about the inherent evil of slavery, Lewis Morris was never moved to manumit his slaves. Accumulating wealth was his powerful and overriding drive.

The influence of the two Lewis Morrises in colonial New Jersey helped create a society wherein owning slaves became deeply entrenched and widely accepted. In effect, they gave their imprimatur to succeeding generations of New Jersey slaveholders who wanted the status and prestige of holding other people in bondage.

The slaves who created vast sums for Morris at Tinton Manor did so through backbreaking labor. Abetted by a few white indentured servants, the slaves worked at the two mills on the property along Falles Creek. A sawmill turned timber culled from the thousands of acres of surrounding forest into lumber for use in the manor and for export to New York markets. A gristmill produced flour from the acres of wheat, rye, barley, oats and corn. The slaves planted, tended and harvested these crops. They were especially skilled from the difficult field labor they performed in the sugar cane fields of Barbados. Seen as efficient and inexpensive machines, the enslaved men were forced to work long hours and days with just enough sustenance to keep them going. Their "negro house" would have been a rudimentary shelter. They probably slept on its dirt floor with hay or straw to ease some of their weariness. That it was within sight of Lewis Morris's grander manor house must have added to their discomfort.

The slaves also became excellent animal husbandmen, tending to Tinton Manor's variety of cattle, pigs and hogs, sheep and horses. Slaves milked the cows, made cheese and butchered the animals for meat. Though the highly skilled ironmongers directing the ironworks at Tinton were free white men, it is certain that most of the dangerous and heavy-duty work for making the valuable bar iron was done by the slaves.

Remarkably, we know quite a bit about one particular enslaved African, Yaff, a man described as the senior Lewis Morris's lifelong "personal servant."

Yaff's African country of origin before he came into Morris's possession is unknown. He might have been born on Barbados to enslaved African parents. Linguists suggest that Yaff is a name common among people from the Senegambia area of Western Africa. Perhaps Yaff or his parents were shipped to Barbados from one of the many slave ports in Senegal or Gambia.

Monmouth University professor Julius Adekunle, a native of Nigeria, speculates, "There are hundreds of languages in Africa. It is therefore difficult to trace the ethnic group the person or the name belonged to. I can say that the name does not seem to be Yoruba. I am not sure how close the name is to Muslim names such as Yesufu or Yusuff or Yasiff. Many slave owners often changed their slaves' names. For example, African slaves in early America were given names such as Coffe or Cuffe, Longo, Moccafunke, Mongo or Zambo. Did Kofi from Ghana transform into Coffe or Cuffe in America? Or, did Lango in Uganda change to Longo?"

Because Lewis Morris chose Yaff to be his personal attendant, the slave must have demonstrated special talents. Perhaps Yaff's physical looks appealed to Morris enough that the young man was rescued from brutal sugar cane field work and brought inside the Morris residence for slightly less demanding work. Maybe Morris's first wife, Ann Barton, chose Yaff to attend to her husband. In any event, Yaff must have been a quick study, learning English and the manners necessary to ingratiate himself with his white master. Yaff stayed at Lewis Morris's side for the remainder of the slaveholder's life. And, as we'll see, Yaff also interacted with many of the early founders and influential men of the colonial period in America. He was evidently a gifted man.

Yaff arrived at Tinton Manor after almost twenty years with Lewis Morris in Barbados. Yaff was just as important to Morris when the slaveholder needed to visit his other properties in New York and Long Island. An old map shows another Morris house on the Swimming River near a "landing place." This depot was just a few miles from the ironworks and plantation. From there, Morris took his sloop down the Navesink River, passed through an inlet on the barrier beach into the Atlantic Ocean and headed north toward New York and Morrisania. Accompanying Morris on these journeys, Yaff might have become an experienced navigator.

When Lewis Morris died, he designated his heir as the nephew who would grow up to become the first royal governor of New Jersey. Among the bequeaths in Morris's final will and testament, dated February 1690–91, is this surprise: "Item. I give and beq[ueath] unto my hon[ore]d friend, William Penn, my negro man Yaff. provided the said Penn shall come to dwell in America; otherwise the said Yaff is to serve my wife equally with other negroes."

Why would Morris leave Yaff to the Quaker founder of Philadelphia? Recall that Lewis Morris had known Penn's father, Admiral Penn, during their time together in the Caribbean theater of the English Civil Wars. The Admiral died in 1670, so at least the gift of Yaff was a debt of gratitude to the Penn family. It was also an inducement to get the younger Penn, then in London, to return to the colonies—a kind of quid pro quo.

Right: William Penn, the founder of Pennsylvania, was a Quaker and a slaveholder. *William Penn portrait by Francis Place, circa 1698.*

Below: Part of "A New Mapp of East and West New Jarsay" by John Thornton of London in 1706. *"A New Mapp of East and West New Jarsay," John Thornton, 1706.*

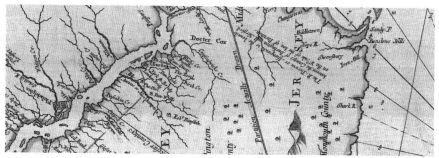

William Penn Jr. was also connected to Morris through George Fox, the founder of the Society of Friends. They had traveled together in England and Ireland while the younger man decided to become a Quaker. Later, William Penn wrote the preface to the *Journal of George Fox*, which described Fox's time with Morris in Barbados. And in 1672, William Penn visited with Lewis Morris at Tinton Manor. The estate was not too far from Philadelphia, a day's carriage ride along the Burlington Path across the narrow midsection of the Jerseys.

William Penn and other prominent Quakers purchased West Jersey in 1677. Arriving in the American colonies five years later, Penn first set about creating a government for the new Province of Pennsylvania. He explored his territory, treated with the resident Lenapes, established plans for Philadelphia on the western shore of the Delaware River and started construction of the Pennsbury Manor estate farther upriver.

Despite the modern popular image of William Penn—benevolent Quaker, friendly and gracious to Native Americans—he was also a slaveholder. According to his biographer, Andrew R. Murphy, "William Penn owned slaves, and displayed no sign of a troubled conscience over it. Even for devout Quakers, the economic gain and luxury derived from the labor of slaves took precedence over an incipient moral scruples about the practice." Penn and Morris were kindred, if sometimes unkind, spirits.

Penn and eleven other proprietors purchased East Jersey from the trustees of Sir George Carteret in February 1682, the same year Lewis Morris was appointed to the East Jersey Council and the Supreme Court. Morris and Penn both attended acting governor Thomas Rudyard's governing council meeting.

William Penn eventually left the colonies for London in the fall of 1684 and stayed in England for the next fifteen years. Lewis Morris hoped he'd see his friend again. This is why, near the end of his life, Morris offered a slave as a bribe for Penn to return to America. Morris didn't live to reunite with his friend, but his heir and nephew saw to it that the old man's final wishes were carried out.

William Penn returned to America in December 1699, a decade after the death of his friend Lewis Morris. Very soon thereafter, the slave Yaff was presented to him, maybe in Philadelphia, or when Penn visited Tinton

---

THE LAST WILL OF LEWIS MORRIS.

Whereas I formerly intended to have made my nephew, Lewis Morris, son of my deceased brother, Richard Morris, my sole executor; his many and great miscarryages and disobedience towards me and my wife, and his causeless absenting himself from my house, and adhering to and advizeing with those of bad life and conversation, contrary to my directions and example unto him, and for other reasons best known to myselfe, I doe make and ordaine my dearly beloved wife, Mary Morris, sole executrix of this my last will and testament; and

To the meeting of Friends at Shrewsberry, in Monmouth Co., five pounds current money of New York per annum forever, to be paid out of his plantation at Tinton iron works, to be paid on 25th March yearly.

Item. I give and beq unto my hon'd friend, *William Penn*, my negro man Yaff, provided the said Penn shall come to dwell in America; otherwise the s'd Yaff is to serve my said wife equally with other negroes. *Item.* I give and beq unto William Bickley one negro girl named Maria. *Item. . . . .* to Wm. Richardson one negro boy named Jack. *Item. . . . .* to Sam'l Palmer one n. girl named Buckey. *Item.* I . . . unto my negro man Toney, the cooper, the sum of 40 shillings a yeare during his life, besides his usual accommodation. *Item. . . . .* unto my negro w'n Nell her ffreedom and liberty to goe att large wheres'r she shall please after the dec'se of my s'd wife. These two last beq'ts are with this restriction and limitation, that they yield all duty, full submis'n and faithf'l obed'ce in all respect as becom'h dilig't serv'ts tow'ds my wife; otherwise, they are to enjoy no benefit hereby, but their beq'ts to be void, as if

This excerpt from Lewis Morris's 1691 last will and testament shows that he bequeathed his slave Yaff to William Penn. History of the County of Westchester, *1848.*

1703.

WILLIAM PENN TO JAMES LOGAN.

LONDON, 1st 2d-mo., 1703.

I have writ at large six sheets if not seven, and sent by R. Mompesson, Esq., to which refer thee. I here inclose Randall Janney's bond for two of his best servants: one a carpenter, the other an husbandman, that the out-houses in part may be perfected within, and a moderate stable built for eight or ten horses, and a shelter for cattle or sheep near the barn,[1] as formerly, to which I refer to J. Sotcher. Yaff is also gone, in the room of one that can't go for weakness, and I have resolved after four years faithful service he shall be free. Yet I have left it to him to return, if he may, passage free (which he will more than deserve in any ship) in the Messenger. Nay, I leave it for him to return from Deal if he will. Thou art to allow R. Janney nothing for him, that goes into the £20 for the other two; also, he wants three of his complement, and must have paid as much had he not gone; besides, I have otherwise been kind to him. Yaff is an able planter and good husbandman, and promises fair, and Samuel has but one year more to serve, I think, by my note, if he has served well. I hope Randall carries a hat for Edward Shippen of a mayoral size: I ordered one for him

See if the town would be so kind to build me a pretty box like Ed. Shippen's, upon any of my lots in town or liberty land, or purchase Griffith Owen's, or T. Fairman's,[2] or any near healthy spot, as Wicaco or the like, for Pennsbury will hardly accommodate my son's family and mine, unless enlarged. Let what is there be kept up, but only substantial improvements to be now followed. I should like fruit at the distance of forty or fifty feet in fields, as also peach-trees; yet shall neither hurt corn nor grass.

Now is the time to make earnings in the islands; wherefore fail not to use the opportunity, and let me see some chests of furs per Messenger. If thou canst, send me per her a copy of the laws to lie by me. Churchill calls on me for his money; pray write and return what is sold, and what I must say to him. I send 2 or 300 books against George Keith, by R. Jenney, which may be disposed of as there is occasion and service; if I have more time I shall write again: so take my leave for this time; Randall going in an hour, and this has three or four miles to go to him. Thy loving friend, WM. PENN.

P. S.— My dear love to all friends, and salutes to all that deserve it. Take care of my mills. Remember me to my family, and let them be kind to poor Lucy and Dutch.

In 1703, William Penn wrote from London to James Logan, his secretary in Philadelphia, that he had freed his slave Yaff. Correspondence between William Penn and James Logan and Others, 1700–1750.

Manor or at governmental meetings in New York. Wherever it happened, Yaff's extraordinary life changed once again. He went back and forth between Philadelphia and Pennsbury Manor, serving Penn during his business dealings in the expanding city and at the country estate.

It is remarkable that a relatively unknown slave worked closely with so many men important to the founding of our country. Yaff spent half a century with the richest man in East Jersey, Colonel Lewis Morris. Yaff met the founder of the Society of Friends, George Fox. Yaff belonged to the first royal governor of New Jersey, Lewis Morris, and was then given to the founder of Pennsylvania, William Penn. Yaff also knew Penn's secretary, the future mayor of Philadelphia, James Logan. And because we know that Yaff made another voyage across the Atlantic Ocean to London toward the end of his life, he undoubtedly met many other movers and shakers of the time.

What became of this man Yaff? We get a last glimpse of his incredible life in an April 1703 letter Penn wrote from London. After Penn had departed America for the last time, he wrote back to his secretary, James Logan. Among business notes, Penn casually mentions, "Yaff. is also gone…& I have resolved after four years of faithfull [*sic*] service he shall be set free. Yet I have left it to him to returne [*sic*] if [he] may passage free (which he will more than deserve in any ship) in the Messenger; nay I leave it for him to return from Deal [the English seaport] if he will.…I have otherwise been kinde [*sic*] to him. Yaff. is an able planter, & good husbandman (and promises faire)."

We can only speculate why Yaff would be at Deal in 1703 and what he might have done next. Did Penn send him to the town at the seaport entry to the Thames River on business or to begin a free new life? Did Yaff rejoin Penn in London? We don't know, but additional research in England might reveal more.

We can hazard some probabilities. In Penn's letter, Yaff sounds hale and hearty. Based on the known timeline of his service to the Morrises, Yaff was between fifty and sixty years old when he got to Deal. At an advanced age for the time, would Yaff have any incentive to return to America, even at Penn's expense? Unless Yaff had a wife and children at Pennsbury or Tinton Manor, it seems unlikely that he would return to the scenes of his enslaved years in the colonies. If he had left Africa as a child, he would have only tenuous connections to his mother country. Because he was skilled, fluent in English and well-connected, it's likely that Yaff lived out his remaining days in England, perhaps buying a home, tending to a garden and even enjoying a domestic relationship. All in all, Yaff lived a most wondrous life.

Have you heard what that mean old judge has done to me?
He told the jury not to let my man go free.
There I stood with my heart so full of misery.
He must die on the gallows, that was the court's decree.
—Ida Cox, *"Last Mile Blues"*

There was yet another Lewis Morris in seventeenth-century Shrewsbury, East Jersey, but his fate was vastly different from his cousin in Tinton Falls.

Lewis Morris of Passage Point (today's Rumson) seems to have been a difficult character for everyone to deal with. He quarreled with his neighbors and appears in early court records for several civic offenses. He was a particularly cruel master to his slaves, and they murdered him in 1695.

This Lewis Morris beat and killed a female slave. When his other slaves were rebuffed in their demands to local courts to bring Morris to justice, they plotted their own revenge. The court had no compunction against bringing these Black men to trial, accusing them of "shooting him through the body with a hand gun." Two slaves—Agebee and Jeremy—were judged guilty and hanged. A third accomplice, Oliver, was whipped. East Jersey courts always acted swiftly to punish the slightest whiff of slave insurrections. Incidents like this and the more serious slave uprisings in New York City (1712) and the West Indies (1760 Jamaica and others) changed at least one aspect of how slaves were acquired. Believing that Caribbean slaves were inherently rebellious, some eighteenth-century slaveholders preferred to buy their chattel directly from Africa.

THOUGH OUR STORY OF New Jersey enslavement is focused on African Americans, we should note that Native American Lenapes, an Algonquian people, were also enslaved and sheltered runaway slaves when they could. Surprisingly, some Lenapes were slaveholders themselves.

During the proprietary period in New Jersey history, the governor and council worried about the relationship between Africans and Indians. In 1682, for instance, it "was agreed and ordered that a message be sent to the Indian sachems to confer with them about their entertainment of negro servants." Fines were established in an effort to keep this intermingling "entertainment" to a minimum. The authorities were clearly worried about potential trouble if the two marginalized and subject people joined forces against white settlers.

WELL INTO THE EARLY nineteenth century, Black men in New Jersey were assumed to be slaves unless they could produce paper as evidence to the contrary. For two centuries, laws and statutes were created to restrict the movement and freedoms of enslaved people. Slaves were constantly suspected of stealing from their masters, and hard penalties were enforced. Ordinary free citizens could whip slaves who they suspected of selling stolen goods. These self-appointed vigilantes might even get financial rewards from the slaves' owners.

Slave behavior was rigidly controlled. They were prohibited from being rude, owning firearms, buying liquor, traveling without permits, organizing meetings, being out past curfew and even setting animal traps. Corporal punishments for offenders ran the horrible gamut from cutting off limbs to burning at the stake. Figurative and literal nooses were continually tightened on slaves. The 1741 New York City slave insurrection, sometimes called the "Great Negro plot," once again filled the white population of New Jersey with dread and fear of uprisings. An 1816 slave rebellion in Barbados, though brutally suppressed, had particular resonance with the remaining New Jersey slaveholders.

Even after they attained freedom, slaves were seen as less than human, as evidenced by the belief that "free negroes are an idle, slothful people and prove very often a charge to the place where they are." From such abhorrent ideas came a 1714 law meant to make manumissions difficult. It required slaveholders to provide £200 to each manumitted slave, plus £20 annually, equivalent to over $50,000 (plus $5,000 yearly) in today's money. This was left in place for seventy years in New Jersey.

In an odd quirk of the law, freed negroes were allowed to vote by the New Jersey State Constitution of 1776. It stated that any inhabitant of the colony of the full age and worth £50 was granted suffrage. The state constitution of 1844 changed this "oversight" to return the franchise to white men only.

DESPITE DISCRIMINATORY LAWS AND oppression, New Jersey slaves acquired a full range of useful skills working for their white owners, as we've seen. They were often more proficient than their oppressors at many jobs. Slaves were farmhands and, according to Summit, New Jersey historian Henry Scofield Cooley, were also "stablemen, coachmen, stage drivers, sailors, boatmen, minors [sic], iron workers, saw mill hands, house and ship carpenters, wheelwrights, coopers, tanners, shoemakers, millers, bakers, cooks" and more. Rutgers historian Giles R. Wright added that male slaves served "as seafarers and dockworkers who drew upon habits found among African groups situated close to bodies of water…other occupations…akin to African work traditions included blacksmithing, weaving, and…fiddling, a talent related to that of professional musicians found among the West African coast."

Slave women, according to Cooley, "became expert at cooking, sewing, spinning and knitting, and worked as maids, barbers, nurses, farm servants, etc." Despite slavery, African Americans were creating a vibrant middle class, though no one would have recognized it as such at the time.

Cooley catalogued page after page of discriminatory laws and two hundred years of atrocious treatment of Black people in *A Study of Slavery in New Jersey*, written in 1889. Nonetheless, he concludes, outrageously: "Slaves were, on the whole, well treated in New Jersey." How can we account for such willful ignorance of shamefully revealed history? Only if we acknowledge that racist attitudes and beliefs trumped all evidence to the contrary for centuries, as they continue to do today.

New Jersey slavery started with chained footholds in Monmouth and Bergen Counties and then spread painfully throughout the rest of the state over the course of two hundred years.

3

SHREWSBURY SLAVERY AND THE REVOLUTIONARY WAR

Standin' at the crossroad, baby, risin' sun goin' down
Standin' at the crossroad, baby, risin' sun goin' down
I believe to my soul, now, poor Bob is sinkin' down
—*Robert Johnson, "Cross Road Blues"*

One hundred years after Lewis Morris brought his slaves to East Jersey, the vile practice of human bondage was firmly established throughout the colony, especially in Monmouth County. No longer the exclusive privilege of the very wealthy, slavery was by then accepted as status quo by yeoman farmers and small merchants alike. We see this starkly illustrated in various lists of slaveholders assembled on the eve of the Revolutionary War.

On December 6, 1769, the General Assembly of the Province of New Jersey passed "an Act to settle the Quotas of the several Counties in this Colony, for the levying Taxes." It stated, "Every bought Servant and Slave, being a Male of Sixteen Years old and upwards, (except such Slaves as are not able to Work) shall be Rated the Sum of Four Shillings."

As colonial resentment for the mother country's taxes intensified, local New Jersey officials initially resisted taking part in any official census of slaves, but they eventually complied. Monmouth County constable Richard Stout compiled an account of adult slaves based on the surveys of auditors in Freehold, Middletown, Shrewsbury, Dover and Stafford. Stout found 536 slaves in total. There were many more, since the surveys excluded minor children under sixteen, slaves beyond their working years or those who were infirm. In 1771, slaves represented 12 percent of a total county population of 11,234, a significant proportional increase.

The tax lists reveal that the number of slaves per owner was in the low single digits, none approaching the hundred-plus slaves the Morris family owned. Slaveholding in colonial New Jersey was the norm and the aspiration of folks making their way up in colonial society.

These 250-year-old lists are stored at the Monmouth County Archives in Manalapan. The slaveholders in Freehold claimed 158 working slaves; 103 in Upper Freehold; 165 in Middletown; 97 in Shrewsbury; 9 in Dover; and 4 in Stafford. Thus the average white slaveholder controlled fewer than 3 slaves, with most having only 1. Slaves were relatively expensive to acquire but provided social status, as well as easing personal labors. The people who appear on these lists were wealthier and seen as more successful by their non-slave-owning neighbors.

Slavery in pre-Revolutionary New Jersey was widely accepted by people of every religious affiliation and occupation. Almost everyone living, working and worshipping at the Four Corners of Shrewsbury Town was a slaveholder. This included Quakers, a Church of England minister, a tavern owner and farmer and a family with deep roots in Monmouth County. These slaveholders were people who would soon take opposite sides in the Revolution. Both Loyalists and future rebels held slaves. The lists feature local government officials, clergymen, farmers and shopkeepers.

Enumerator and "Constobel" Asher West wrote at the top of his Shrewsbury list, in his unlettered crude language, "July 23, 1771. An account of All the Neger Slaves & melatos both Men & Women as near as I Can find in Shrewsbury." West found fifty-eight individuals holding a total of ninety-nine slaves. (He amended his final accounting, noting that two slaves were already on the Freehold list, to a corrected total of ninety-seven.)

The majority of these slaveholders, thirty of them, owned only one slave. Seventeen owned two, seven had three and four claimed to own four slaves. We can identify twenty or so of these slaveholders from historical records.

The Shrewsbury slaveholder list reveals just how commonplace slavery was. The very heart of Shrewsbury Town, then as now, is the Four Corners—the intersection of the Eatontown Turnpike (Broad Street) and the road to Tinton Falls (Sycamore Avenue). Facing each other across this intersection were John Wardell's house, the Blue Ball Tavern, the Quaker Meeting and Christ Church. The Presbyterian church was just down Sycamore Avenue. We might think of the intersection as the Four Corners of Slavery.

July 4 23th 1771 an Acount of All the Neger Slave & melater both
men & Woman as near as I Can find In Shrewsbury

Parson Ashfield	2	Joseph Fleman	1
Rebekah West	2	Ritchard Cole	3
Nicklous Vanbrount	1	Mary Marton	1
Nicklous Vanbrount Juner	1	James Corlis	1
Ritchard Lordnce	1	William Parker son of Joseph	1
Stephen Tallman Juner	2	Samuel Breef	3
John Wardill	3	John Corlis	4
Joseph Price	1	John Hartfon	2
Jesiah Hetter	2	Morris Dehart	2
James Smith	2	Jesiah Parker	2
Margret Boundley	1	Joseph Wardill son of Jacob	1
Joseph Wardill son of Sam	1	Jorge Toyler	1
John Williams son of Danl	1	Lucy Eton	1
Joseph Lenard	2	Isaack Harber	2
Cooper Wardill Juner	2	Juke Wacoff	2
John Wardill Cotman	1	Benjaman Vannrter	4
John Selearn	1	Mical Hanney	4
Peter Parker	1	John Hehemous	2
Jacob Wardill	2	Cornelious Vandevear	3
John Morris	3	Levy Hort	1
Samuel Tucker	1	Joseph Throgmorton	2
Robert Hervy	1	Asher Toyler	1
Samuel Cook	4	Thomas Hankison	1
Thomas Morford	1	Abraham Pebasho	1
James West	1	Joseph Jonson	1
David Knott	3	John Garmage	1
John Littel	2	Samuel Lenard	2
Samuel Tallman	1	John Maires	1
Elihu Williams	1		51
James Boggs	1	Asher West Constabel	48
	48		99
		Joseph Lenard given in Toolate	2
			97

This 1771 Shrewsbury slave list was created in response to New Jersey's General Assembly law requiring an inventory of all enslaved people. *Monmouth County Archives.*

110. *The New-York Gazette; or, The Weekly Post-Boy*, #580, March 11, 1754.

Run away the 10th of January last, from John Wardell of Shrewsbury, a small Negro Fellow named Ash; he took with him a red Duffil Watch-coat, good bearskin Under-Coat, Camblet Jacket and Kersey Breeches with Brass Buckles on them. Whoever takes up and secures said Man, so that his Master may have him again, shall have Forty Shillings Reward and all reasonable charges paid, by John Wardell.

Top: An eighteenth-century sketch of the Shrewsbury Town "Four Corners" shows (*left to right*) the Blue Ball Tavern, a blacksmith shop, the Quaker Meeting and Christ Church. *Shrewsbury Historical Society*.

Bottom: This 1754 ad in the *New York Gazette* is typical of the kind slaveholders like Shrewsbury's John Wardell would place in an attempt to recover their runaway slaves, here a man named Ash. *The* New York Gazette *via Newspapers.com*.

Wardells were among the earliest settlers in Monmouth County. In 1771, John Wardell owned forty acres of land at the southwest corner. The property—a "great house" with surrounding farmland—required slave labor to keep it running. Wardell owned three slaves, and like most of his prominent family, he was a Quaker. Although contemporary Quakers were beginning to free their slaves in their last wills and testaments, John Wardell does not appear to have been so enlightened. He was eventually "read out" of the Shrewsbury Meeting.

Some years earlier, in 1754, Wardell took out an ad in a New York newspaper offering a reward for a runaway named Ash, "a small Negro fellow." As in many similar ads of the time, Wardell described exactly what Ash was wearing: his "red Duffil Watch-coat, good bearskin Under-Coat, Camblet Jacket and Kersey Breeches with Brass Buckles." Why such detail? Ash's decision to escape was probably unplanned and spontaneous, and the runaway fled with just the clothes on his back. Wardell hoped that if Ash got to New York, someone would recognize his distinctive outfit and return the man in exchange for a forty-shilling reward. There is no record that anyone claimed it.

In July 1776, John's cousin Joseph Wardell joined John Corlies (whose relationship with a particular slave was noteworthy, as we'll see) and George Allen on a trip to Staten Island to retrieve three runaway slaves. During the Revolutionary War, the Wardells remained fiercely loyal to the British Crown. John Wardell would pay a high price for that loyalty. The Council and General Assembly of New Jersey had passed "an Act for forfeiting to and vesting in the State of New Jersey the real Estates of certain Fugitives and offenders." The properties of many Monmouth County citizens were taken from those who chose to remain allied with King George III. John Wardell's real estate was appropriated and sold at auction in March 1779. The Commission of Forfeited Estates granted it to William M. Lippincott for £4,410.

THE FIFTY-SIX-ACRE FARM AND orchard opposite the Wardell estate, just on the other side of the Tinton Falls Road, was owned by Josiah Halstead in 1771. Identified by its distinctive sign, the well-known establishment was known as the Blue Ball Tavern, operated by the notoriously difficult man. Halstead had frequent legal problems involving failure to pay taxes and other matters. He took three wives over his time in Shrewsbury and seemed always on the brink of bankruptcy.

Halstead was a harsh slave master, as evidenced by several ads he took out about his runaways, including one mentioning an indentured servant. Two Halstead slaves are on the Shrewsbury list, though he certainly owned others. He tried, on several occasions, to sell his tavern and farm. In a 1768 notice of sale, he described his properties and then, in an afterthought, wrote, "N.B. One or more likely Negro boys to be sold, at private sale, the same time, or before, who can be well recommended." In this context, "likely" meant promising and good workers.

ON THE NORTHWEST CORNER of the Four Corners intersection were the meetinghouse and cemetery of the Society of Friends. Although Quakers are now popularly thought of as avid abolitionists, this was not always the case. Just like their contemporaries, Quakers often owned slaves. As Quaker Meetings debated the merits of slavery and moved toward an abolitionist position, some Friends granted enslaved "servants" freedom in their wills. More than a few Quakers manumitted older slaves (seen as worn out and therefore less valuable) while bequeathing younger and healthier slaves to their children. (It's not much of a stretch to imagine these men on their deathbeds "trying to get to heaven before they close the door," as Bob Dylan would sing a few centuries later.)

The Shrewsbury Meeting opposed the importation of slaves to New Jersey as early as 1730, though it took years for all of the Quakers to adhere to the precept. Some refused. In 1757, the meeting disowned John Wardell for buying a slave. A year later, members of the meeting were asked to stop buying slaves, to teach literacy to slave children and to free them at the age of twenty-one. Despite these remonstrances, many Quakers resisted manumitting their slaves. Related by marriage to the Wardells, four Parker slaveholders are also on the list.

Perhaps the Shrewsbury Quaker most resistant to abolition was John Corlies. He owned four slaves who he'd inherited from his father. His widowed mother, Zilpha, owned two slaves. John Corlies's resistance to evolving Quaker principles regarding slavery was key to the story of the most famous runaway slave in Revolutionary New Jersey history.

Corlies treated his slaves abominably, beat them for the slightest transgressions and refused to educate them. Representatives of the Quaker Meeting visited his home more than once to discuss this treatment of his slaves. These visits were typical of how Quakers exercised their religious and moral beliefs. Persuasive discussions, rather than direct admonitions, were thought to be an effective way to bring straying or errant Friends back into the fold. But John Corlies would not be convinced to manumit his slaves. He was quite strident when he told Quaker elders that "he has not seen it his duty to give [the slaves] their freedom." Eventually, the meeting disowned Corlies, as they had John Wardell.

———

Got a boy-child's comin',
He's gonna be a son-of-a-gun.
— McKinley Morganfield, also known as Muddy Waters,
"Hoochie Coochie Man"

One of John Corlies's slaves, a twenty-year-old named Titus, might have overheard these Quaker discussions and realized that his situation was not going to improve. In early November 1775, Titus ran away from Corlies, who soon advertised for his capture and return. Although Titus would not have known about it on the day he escaped, an offer of freedom from the British royal governor of Virginia provided him with an extraordinary opportunity to seek revenge. Hundreds of New Jersey slaves would also run away once word spread to them about this offer. It's estimated that as many as 100,000 slaves left their colonial masters by the end of the Revolution, in what's been called "the largest Black escape in the history of North American slavery."

John Murray, Earl of Dunmore and colonial governor of Virginia, issued a proclamation on November 7, 1775, declaring, "All indentured Servants, Negroes, or others (appertaining to Rebels) free, that are able and willing to

THREE POUNDS Reward.

RUN away from the subscriber, living in Shrewsbury, in the county of Monmouth, New-Jersey, a NEGROE man, named Titus, but may probably change his name; he is about 21 years of age, not very black, near 6 feet high; had on a grey homespun coat, brown breeches, blue and white stockings, and took with him a wallet, drawn up at one end with a string, in which was a quantity of clothes. Whoever takes up said Negroe, and secures him in any goal, or brings him to me, shall be entitled to the above reward of *Three Pounds* proc. and all reasonable charges, paid by

Nov. 8, 1775. § JOHN CORLIS.

When John Corlies advertised for his runaway slave Titus, he could not have foreseen that the man would return to Monmouth County as a terrorist working for the British. *The* New York Gazette *via Newspapers.com.*

bear Arms, they joining his Majesty's Troops." Dunmore and other British officials thought the pesky little colonial rebellion would be put down quickly, especially if the rebels lost their enslaved labor force.

How did Titus escape the clutches of his master, John Corlies, to sign on with Dunmore's Ethiopian Regiment to fight with the British? Although we don't have documentary evidence of his methods and route, we can speculate.

At almost six feet tall and apparently well put together, Titus would have a hard time escaping notice while he was on the run. Corlies's ad says Titus was "not very black," a "mulatto" in contemporary eighteenth-century terms, and his light-skinned visage could have helped a bit. Nonetheless, a Black man traveling by himself without a written pass from his owner would put Titus at considerable risk.

New York City, forty miles or so north of Shrewsbury, was tantalizingly within reach for Titus. There he could blend in with a population of free Blacks or disguise himself as one of the many sailors of varying nationalities coming and going through the busy seaport. Anyone sympathetic to his plight could provide food and shelter. Temporary work at night in the busy city's many taverns, bawdyhouses or illegal trading businesses was possible. Once the news of Dunmore's proclamation reached the port, Titus could sign onto a ship's crew or even stow away to get to Virginia to take advantage of Dunmore's offer. But New York was still a long walk or a few days' carriage ride away—doable, but hazardous.

The easiest and most obvious safe haven for Titus was within sight of his enslavement. John Corlies lived on Rumson Neck at what was called Black Point. The Corlies family had been there for years. The barrier beach leading to Sandy Hook—due east of Corlies's property—was one hundred yards or so across the Shrewsbury River. All Titus had to do was take a small boat across the river at night and then walk north under cover of darkness. All types of boats on the Shrewsbury River took agricultural produce and other goods between Monmouth County and New York. John Corlies might have owned one.

If Titus needed help, he could turn to the Quakers, who had tried to convince Corlies and his mother to manumit their slaves. Titus knew these Friends and might have discussed an escape plan with them. A document filed after the war by two Loyalist brothers suggests such an alternative for Titus.

In 1784, Robert and Esek Hartshorne requested compensation from Parliament for cedar timber taken from their Sandy Hook property by the British army. As a Quaker elder, Robert had actually met with John Corlies about the latter's slaves some years before. Robert lived on Portland

Titus escaped from the Corlies property on Rumson Neck (*left background*) to Sandy Hook (*foreground*). The Quaker Hartshornes, living north of the Navesink River (*center*), might have helped him. *Wikimedia Commons.*

Road in Middletown, just across the Navesink River and not too far from John Corlies. Esek's house was near Buttermilk Hollow Road, also in Middletown. Titus might have found his way to one of these safe houses on his way to British-controlled and Hartshorne-owned Sandy Hook. John Hartshorne, another brother, was a neighbor of John Corlies. So, Titus had potential help close by. There was precedent for runaways like him to follow this path to freedom.

The *New York Gazette* printed the following on November 7, 1763: "About three weeks ago, a Negro Man came to the House of Thomas Letson, at Black-Point, in East New Jersey. He calls himself Sambo is about 5½ feet high, speaks English very indifferently, says he belongs to one Allen; and is now very sick. Whoever lays Claim to said Negro, and proves Property, may have him, (on paying charges) by applying to the said Thomas Letson."

Sambo was apprehended, and probably returned to Allen. But Titus and other slaves were very aware of these escape attempts—their masters made sure they saw the subsequent punishments for those recaptured—but the slaves also learned what to do and what not to do when their own opportunities to run away came along.

In August 1776, ten months after Titus ran away from John Corlies, British troops occupied densely populated New York, a city of twenty thousand or so people. If Titus had made it from Sandy Hook to New York, he might have volunteered to fight against the colonial rebels and his former owner, taken a British naval ship bound for Norfolk, Virginia, and trained with Lord Dunmore's Ethiopian Regiment.

The British would have quickly recognized Titus's fierce determination for revenge against Corlies, and they certainly could find use for his knowledge of Monmouth County. Calling himself Colonel Tye (a military honorific but perhaps also a direct rebuke to Corlies's ad, which suggested the runaway "may probably change his name"), the one-time slave would become the scourge of Monmouth County rebels. He fought with the British in the pivotal Battle of Monmouth in June 1778, during which he captured a Patriot militia captain. (What must Tye have thought when he saw almost two hundred African Americans and Native Americans fighting on the side of the rebellious colonials during that crucial battle? Those men of color were likely just as astonished to see him in a position of command on the Loyalist side.)

The so-called Black Pioneers were encamped at Refugeetown on Sandy Hook, along with other British troops and hundreds of civilian Loyalists. The British controlled the Hook, which was then an island, so they could ensure their ships had safe passage into New York harbor. The Black Pioneers were sheltered in a conglomeration of huts and tents in the shadow of the Sandy Hook Lighthouse. From that base of operations, Colonel Tye led many raiding parties, rowing across Sandy Hook Bay to wreak havoc on the rebels in coastal New Jersey. Tinton Falls and Shrewsbury were frequent targets.

During 1779 and 1780, Tye led more than a dozen such alarming raids. In charge of a mix of Black and white irregulars, Tye pillaged and burned houses and farms, confiscated cattle and horses, took important militia captives and generally terrified Monmouth County.

Imagine the horror evoked as armed Black men, with years of grievances to avenge, ravaged the countryside during night-time guerrilla operations. Typical of newspaper reports about Tye was this one from June 1780: "The noted Colonel Tye (a mulatto formerly a slave in Monmouth County) with his motley company of about twenty blacks and whites, carried off prisoners Capt. Barney Smock, and Gilbert Van Mater, spiked an iron cannon and took four horses. Their rendezvous was at Sandy Hook."

A few weeks later, Tye was part of another raiding party of "30 blacks, 36 Queen's Rangers, and 30 refugee tories," which plundered several houses and kidnapped at least ten men, "also several Negroes and a great deal of stock." Like Tye, these "Negroes" were probably also Dunmore's People.

During a September 1780 raid at the Colts Neck home of famed rebel leader Joshua Huddy, Tye was among the "72 men, composed of New-Levies, Refugees and Negroes" laying siege. Tye was wounded by a shot to his wrist and died of blood poisoning within a few days. Though Tye never encountered his nemesis John Corlies (who outlived the war), the rebels' relief at the news of Tye's death must have been palpable. Viewing

Freehold's David Forman wrote this letter to General George Washington, describing the capture of Captain Barnes Smock by Colonel Tye and his men, the "Black Pioneers." *Monmouth County Historical Association.*

Tye's actions from today's vantage point, of course, one man's terrorist is another's freedom fighter.

An interesting postscript to these Revolutionary War events involves the Corlies family again. John Corlies died in 1786, but his slaveholding mother, Zilpha, continued to live at Black Point for another sixteen years, until her death. Sometime during the intervening years, Zilpha apparently had a change of heart about her slaves. In a July 1802 letter, her grandson Samuel

Runaway slaves working for the British during the Revolution sometimes wore uniforms emblazoned with "Liberty to Slaves." *Wikimedia Commons.*

Corlies wrote to an attorney for probate advice, saying, "Zilpha Corlies, many years before her death, manumitted a negro woman, and a negro man. The woman is very aged and unable to support herself, and the man, it is probable, before many years will be in the same situation." This old woman was likely the "negro Wench called Sarah," a woman Zilpha inherited from her husband in 1760.

Samuel Corlies's concern was less about the welfare of the slaves than it was about the effects of their manumission on his family. He asked the lawyer, "What steps will be proper for the Executor to take in order to secure their maintenance? Is the estate liable for the support of the children of this black woman born after the manumission of the mother? Who is to take charge of the old woman? Can the legatees forcibly take her out of the hands of the Executor and dispose of her at their discretion?"

The questions suggest that the old Quaker Zilpha Corlies might finally have understood the human cost of enslavement and freed her bondspeople. But they also indicate that the slaves continued to live with Corlies, no doubt for minimal compensation, such as room and board in exchange for their services. Zilpha Corlies got the better part of that deal for freedom.

In typical legalese, attorney Richard Stockton replied to Samuel Corlies:

The Estate of Zilpha Corlies is certainly liable to maintain the old negro manumitted by her—but not the children born while the parent was in a State of Freedom. If the Executor Settles the Estate and pays it over to those entitled to it, he can never be called on for such maintenance, but those having the Estate will be liable thus for. I do not think the Executor has a right to sustain any part of the Estate in his hand on this account. Of course when he part with it he had better let the negro go with the Legatees. They have no right forcible to take away the negro, but they may call the Estate out of the hand of the Executor and be forced to maintain her unless she is permitted to be with them.

When the boatmen stole the Africans
Did your God ride or row?
When they roped 'em and they shackled 'em
Was he with them in the hold?
Was the ocean moon so beautiful
That it brought him to his knees?
What did your God see?
—Eric Taylor, "Your God"

Returning to our examination of slavery at the Four Corners of Shrewsbury Town, the southeast portion of the intersection was, and remains, the site of Christ Church. This second edifice was completed in 1769 due to the efforts of the Reverend Samuel Cooke of the Society for the Propagation of the Gospel in Foreign Parts (SPG).

Cooke owned four slaves on the 1771 tax list. How a poorly paid clergyman acquired these slaves is a story of a man with noble intentions and ignoble audacity.

In 1751, the SPG, the missionary arm of the Church of England, sent Cooke to minister to Shrewsbury in the New Jersey colony. Within two months of his arrival, he wrote back to the secretary of the SPG, "I have baptized five adults, two white children between six and seven years of age, five Negro children, and fifteen infants." He filed years of similar reports, updating the society on his successes in increasing the membership of the church as he continued to spread the word.

A number of Cooke's original handwritten sermon books are now at the Monmouth County Historical Association in Freehold. One is titled *The Duty of Mutual Love Inforced from Our Lord's Example*. Mutual love might have encouraged Samuel Cooke to baptize slaves, but that love did not prevent him from owning his own.

Five years after he arrived in America, Samuel Cooke married Graham Kearney, a granddaughter of the deceased royal governor of New Jersey Lewis Morris. The marriage was a step up in social class for Cooke and enhanced his position with the wealthy parishioners of Christ Church.

The new couple settled into the parish glebe in nearby Leedsville. The glebe was "church farm property," a perk provided by the SPG to supplement the minister's meager salary. Samuel Cooke was a peripatetic preacher, constantly on his rounds to parishioners in Shrewsbury, Middletown and Freehold.

Left: The Church of England's Reverend Samuel Cooke traveled by horseback to churches in Monmouth County to preach. Almost a dozen notebooks of his handwritten sermons are preserved. *Monmouth County Historical Association.*

Below: Samuel Cooke baptized many slaves at Christ Church in Shrewsbury, including those of his sister-in-law Isabella Kearney. *Christ Church, Shrewsbury, New Jersey.*

A few months before his marriage, Cooke baptized five slaves belonging to his future sister-in-law, "Miss Isabella Kearny [sic]." Christ Church parish records indicate that the slaves were "Rachel An Adult Negro Servant" and her four children, Mary, Margaret, Johnson and Bella. There is no mention of the father of the children. Perhaps Isabella Kearney inherited them as slaves from her grandmother Isabella Morris, who died in 1752. As we've seen, the Morris family had dozens of slaves working on their Tinton Falls estate. Isabella Kearney hadn't inherited very much else from her father, Michael, at his death in 1741. Her brothers enjoyed most of his bequeaths.

In 1762, Samuel Cooke, together with his sister-in-law Isabella Kearney, purchased a one-hundred-acre property in a remote and underpopulated area ten miles southwest of Shrewsbury Town, in the little village of Squancum. (Author's note: I live on part of the Cooke/Kearney property today.) Perhaps the Reverend Cooke was being kind to his wife's sister, a forty-six-year-old spinster, so that she'd have a small farm to produce some income. With no husband to help, Isabella needed slaves to manage the property. Her still extant house (in what is now Farmingdale) has an upstairs loft, accessible by a spiral staircase behind the fireplace, probably where the slaves slept.

Samuel and Graham Cooke bought a Shrewsbury farm of 165 acres two years later. The busy preacher Samuel Cooke didn't have time to run two farms and a glebe. His wife needed help with her four children, and she'd eventually have five more. Since Samuel Cooke retained half interest in the 100-acre Squankum farm, the obvious solution would be to transfer some slaves to work at his newer farm.

In August 1766, an entry in the Christ Church registry documents that Isabella Kearney brought four more Black children for baptism: Dinah, Daniel, Chloe and Phillis. The date of this baptism is close enough to Cooke's 165-acre purchase to suggest that Isabella Kearney bought new slaves as replacements for the four Cooke took to his new farm. There is no indication that the four slaves baptized in 1766 were children of the aforementioned Rachel.

Graham Cooke died during the birth of her tenth child in November 1771. The four slaves owned by Samuel Cooke on the Shrewsbury list of the previous July might have been Rachel's children from 1756 or else the four noted in the subsequent baptism.

How to explain eight known Kearney/Cooke slaves but only four on the list? Since Isabella Kearney is not on the list, some of the slaves might have been sold or died or given to other relatives. We can't know for sure, but we're fortunate to have the names of these people who'd otherwise be forgotten to history.

As it turned out, Samuel Cooke's presence in New Jersey as an enthusiastic representative of the Church of England put him in serious jeopardy during the Revolutionary War. He said he was forced to flee to England "on account of threats…hoping that the Confusion in the Colonies would subside." He returned to America in 1776 to take a position as chaplain to the Brigade of Guards in New York City. But he wasn't able to visit Shrewsbury to see his children because New Jersey considered him a fugitive, subject to arrest by the Patriot authorities. He suffered material losses as well.

All of Reverend Cooke's property was auctioned—his house, furniture, books, barn, stables, livestock, farm equipment and slaves. The directive to the sheriff of Monmouth County read:

> *New Jersey pursuant to Law against Samuel Cook* [sic] *late of the Township of Shrewsburry* [sic]*, on an Inquisition found against the Said Samuel Cook for Joining the Army of the King of Great Britain and otherwise offending against his Allegiance to the Said….You are therefore commanded and enjoined to Sell and dispose of all the Estate, Real of what nature or Kind So ever belonging or lately belonging to the Said Samuel Cook within the Said County of Monmouth, according to the Directions of an Act for Forfeiting to and vesting in the State of New Jersey the real Estates of certain Fugitives and offenders made and passed the eleventh Day of December in the Year of our Lord 1778.*

Like many of the Loyalists who suffered the forfeiture of their property, Cooke petitioned Parliament after the war to redress his losses. In addition to asking for reimbursement of the value of his confiscated real estate, Cooke, exhibiting the temerity of a typical slaveholder, asked for compensation for the losses of "a Negro man about 23 years old (£100) and a Negro Wench (£56)." Could these have been the slaves Johnson and one of his sisters, whom Cooke had baptized at Christ Church years earlier? Possibly, because a twenty-three-year-old negro man of 1779 would have been born in 1756, the year Johnson was baptized.

The British Parliament did reimburse Samuel Cooke. Cooke joined thousands of defeated and disheartened American colonial Loyalists who left for British-controlled territory north of the newly emerging United States after the war. He and several of his children landed in New Brunswick, Canada, where he set about organizing new Anglican parishes. While working with unflagging dedication to saving souls, the Reverend Samuel Cooke drowned there in a canoeing accident in 1795.

A slave-related addendum to the Samuel Cooke saga concerns his one-time Shrewsbury Christ Church vestryman Josiah Holmes. Holmes disagreed with Cooke's design of a new Christ Church building because he thought this building was "too fancy and too refined." They argued, and Holmes resigned from the vestry in a fit of pique on Easter Tuesday 1769.

But before his disagreement with Holmes, Samuel Cooke sponsored two drawings to raise funds for the construction of the new church. The drawings were held on an island in the Delaware River because New Jersey had passed a law against lotteries. Recently discovered in the library of an old house across Broad Street from Christ Church, one of the original four-dollar lottery tickets bears the signature of Josiah Holmes. The ticket is number 1369, indicating that hundreds of parishioners purchased lottery chances. A handwritten note on the reverse side, "Also Demand Sampson Sampson's Prises [sic]," probably refers to a slave owned by Holmes. Holmes must have purchased multiple tickets and thought that if he collected on one, he could also cash in a second winner using Sampson's name.

This lottery ticket to raise funds for a new Christ Church was sold to Josiah Holmes in 1758. He wrote on the back that he "also demand" any winnings of his slave Sampson Sampson. *Shrewsbury Historical Society.*

Josiah Holmes, apparently not one to let go of a grudge, testified against the Reverend Cooke during the legal proceedings that led to the Anglican minister losing his property. Holmes also took over Cooke's Christ Church glebe when the missionary left Monmouth County in 1775, yet more salt in Samuel Cooke's considerably painful wartime wounds.

There are twenty-four other Anglicans on the 1771 Shrewsbury tax list, including another Christ Church vestryman, Thomas Morford, the son-in-law of Josiah Holmes. Although Morford owned only one slave, he descended from a multigenerational family of slaveholders. The Christ Church parish records show that a Mrs. Morford, probably Thomas's mother, Hester, had "Elizabeth, a negro woman," baptized in 1751. It would be another sixty-seven years before the Morford family would finally cease holding fellow human beings in bondage.

When Thomas Morford's son Garrett freed a slave in 1818, the manumission document for Samuel Williams stated that he was "of the age of 32 years or thereabouts." This means that when Williams was born, around 1786, Garrett was only five, too young to be a slaveholder. Garrett freed Williams five months after his father, Thomas, died in May 1818. Thomas had owned Samuel Williams. So, Samuel Williams, born after the 1771 list was created, might have been the son of Elizabeth.

———— ◆ ————

THE LAST SLAVE-CONNECTED PROPERTY near the Four Corners in Shrewsbury Town was on Sycamore Avenue, adjacent to Christ Church. Parishioners of the Presbyterian Church were slaveholders too. David Knott, who owned three slaves, was associated with many of the people on the 1771 tax list. They were his neighbors, friends and business associates. David and his father, Peter, were elders and trustees of the Presbyterian Church. The prosperous Knotts had acquired huge tracts of Monmouth County land.

By 1739, Peter Knott had a sawmill on his plantation homestead, which was a few miles from Squancum. His son David built his own Squancum sawmill just where the road to Tinton Falls crosses Mingamahone Brook. These mills were little more than sheds covering waterwheels powered by streams. Mills were labor intensive and operated by slaves. David Knott's slaves cut the timber on his property for the mill, yielding him more crop land. David Knott's sawmill property adjoined Isabella Kearney's

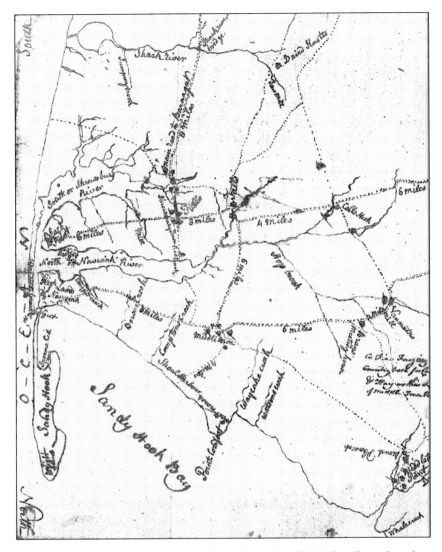

This "Fine Foraging Country" map was probably drawn by a British Loyalist to show the best places to conduct raids in Monmouth County. *Monmouth County Historical Association.*

hundred-acre farm. We've seen how this unmarried woman was able to wrest modest profits from her land with the help of a few slaves.

Knott also owned a tavern at the key intersection in Squancum, just opposite Kearney's home. The pair would have good reasons to help each other and eventually formed a partnership. In 1779, taking advantage of the Loyalist confiscation, they bought Samuel Cooke's half of the one hundred acres where Kearney lived. Isabella Kearney also might have sold David Knott some of her slaves to work on their jointly owned farm.

According to archival historian Michael Adelberg, David Knott was a bit of a "trimmer," meaning he trimmed his political sails according to which way the wind—Patriot or Loyalist—was blowing. Though he had been a member of the rebellious Shrewsbury Committee of Observation with Josiah Holmes, Knott seems to have taken ambiguous stances during the Revolution; there's a big difference between protesting government policies and actively rebelling against that government. Knott was accused in a Monmouth County court of selling supplies to the British on Sandy Hook.

David Knott's home on the estate he inherited from his father, Peter, appears on a roughly drafted 1776 map. Adelberg suggests "A Fine Foraging Country" was "a map prepared by New Jersey Loyalists to show the best places to conduct raids near Sandy Hook. I assume Knott's house (and his sawmill, both shown at the upper right on the map) is listed as a safe house for Loyalist raiding parties. Despite his apparent disloyalty, Knott kept himself out of serious trouble and finished the war among the county's wealthier men, owning more than 300 acres, 2 mills, and 26 horses & cows—a very high number in a region where many lost their livestock to Loyalist raiding parties." David Knott owned plenty of slaves to keep all of his business interests running smoothly.

When he died in 1788, at age fifty-five, David Knott was a bitter old man. He had alienated himself from his neighbors over property feuds. The Monmouth County Orphans Court allocated his landholdings to his children. Although he was an elder in the Presbyterian church in Shrewsbury Town, he was not interred there with his parents. David Knott was buried alone on his farm next to a small stream that eventually becomes the Shark River on its way to the Atlantic Ocean.

During the late eighteenth century, the antislavery movement was increasingly led by the Quakers advocating abolition. Their position was clearly a perceived threat to longtime slaveholders. One activist Quaker, William Dillwyn, wrote, "The prejudices of custom are strong—those imbibed from interest, yet stronger."

In February 1774, thirty-nine prominent Shrewsbury men signed *The Petition of Sundrie of the Inhabitants Freeholders and Owners of Negroes in Shrewsbury.*

These members of the gentry, already worried about reports that slaves were stealing horses, running around at night and congregating at the homes of freed Blacks, were fearful of any new laws granting wider freedom of movements to the enslaved. And they were very afraid that their slaves would rebel and take arms and revenge their status of bondage.

The Revolutionary War was fought against the background of cries for freedom from Britain, the mother country an ocean away from New Jersey. At the same time, concerns about slaves rising up for their own freedom were never far from the minds of colonial slaveholders. In 1775, the Shrewsbury Committee of Correspondence ordered "all arms in the hands of or at the command of negroes, slave or free, shall be taken and secured by the militia officers." The fear of potential slave rebellions was fueled by reports of "numerous and riotous meetings of negroes at unlicensed houses."

AND WHAT OF THE Black Loyalists from New Jersey and other colonies who fled their masters to join the British army? Sometimes called Dunmore's People, they were just as disappointed at the outcome of the Revolutionary War as the British. The fate of these slaves was mixed. Some were returned to Africa (the Sierra Leone Company resettled four thousand to Freetown); some went to England (where they lived with other "Black Poor" in London);

Thousands of Black Loyalists relocated to Nova Scotia after the Revolutionary War. They supported themselves with the same kinds of manual labor they had performed as slaves before the war. *Wikimedia Commons.*

and still others headed to the Caribbean West Indies, Jamaica and the Bahamas (where they were greeted with suspicion and discrimination).

As many as three thousand former slaves boarded British ships in New York bound for resettlement with white Loyalists in Nova Scotia. All too familiar with hardship, these Blacks established new lives for themselves using the skills they learned while enslaved. Many wound up in Shelborne and Birchtown, south of Halifax.

Were these defeated Black collaborators really British Loyalists? Perhaps from a military perspective they were, but their true loyalty was always to attain their freedom from slavery. From that viewpoint, they used the British as a means to an end, as they had been used by their slave masters for generations.

The unluckiest of all of Dunmore's People were those recaptured by slave traders and sold back into slavery. They were punished harshly by vengeful Patriots for having served the British cause—frying pan to fire and back, it seems.

4

SLAVES OF FREEHOLD, HOLMDEL AND MIDDLETOWN

Another hard day, no water, no rest
I saw my chance, so I got him at last
I took his six shooter, put two in his chest
He'll never say a word no more
Oh, he'll never say a word no more
The devil got him good for sure.
—*JJ Julius Son, also known as* KALEO, *"Broken Bones"*

The early citizens of the oldest townships in Monmouth County participated in the sustained abuse of enslaved Africans. The earliest record of a slave execution in East Jersey occurred in 1691. Caesar, owned by James Melven, was tried and convicted of murdering a Mary Wright. The slave was publicly executed on Kings Highway, the historic center of the town.

At least three other slaves were convicted of various crimes and hanged in Middletown during the next several years. Among these was Jeremy, who killed his master, Lewis Morris of Passage Point, now Rumson.

Jeremy was angry at Morris's murder of a female slave, so he and several other slaves shot Morris. Captured and held at "the Middletown gaol" (jail), Jeremy escaped in February 1695. He was caught again and tried. The details of his sentencing are gruesome: "Jeremy, though must go to the place of execution where thy right hand shall be cut off and burnt before thine eyes, then thou shalt be hanged up by the neck until thou art dead, dead, dead; then thy body shalt be cut down and thrown into the fire and burnt to ashes."

The man who recaptured Jeremy was rewarded with a bounty of twenty pounds, a huge sum for that time. These kinds of brutal punishments were designed not just to punish the wrongdoers, but also to hammer home the message to all slaves that they'd better behave and to remind them that they had no rights.

UNJUST BRITISH TAXES AND other legislative actions that rebellious citizens saw as affronts to their colonial way of life were the leading causes of the Revolutionary War. These patriotic rebels were further enraged when the British offered to free any runaway slaves who joined the mother country's military forces. New Jersey citizens who took up arms were often also slaveholders intent on maintaining their human "property," no matter their sincere belief in liberty and freedom.

One of these was Colonel David Rhea (1740–1821) of Freehold, who participated in the 1778 Battle of Monmouth. The pivotal fight was mostly fought on the farm inherited from his father, also David Rhea. Colonel Rhea knew the topology of the battlefield so well that he advised George Washington where to mount his artillery. David Rhea Sr.'s will of 1761 bequeathed slaves named Frank, Liss, Lydia, Titus, Bristol and Sarah to his wife and children. David Rhea Jr. inherited an enslaved man named Umple.

After the war, David Rhea became sheriff of Monmouth County in 1785. He continued to own slaves, at least one of whom was of mixed heritage. A Rhea slave is referenced in a September 1791 ad in a Philadelphia newspaper, ironically named *Freeman's Journal*.

The runaway was:

> an indented Indian mulatto boy, named Israel Tolmen, whose father was a white man, and mother an Indian; by profession a chimney sweeper, and about nineteen years of age, five feet nine or ten inches high, hallow face, and very slender made, black short hair hangs above his neck, with brown eyes….He formerly lived with Col. Ray [sic], and Mr. Samuel Turman at Monmouth in Jersey, and is capable of telling a good tale, and has travelled much through the Jersey, and was born in Allen Town. Whoever takes up said runaway and secures him in any gaol, so that his master gets him again, shall receive the above reward ["Four Dollars"], and reasonable charges.

Four Dollars Reward.

RAN away from the Subscriber living in Dock-street, Nº 59, on Sunday the 11th inst. an indented Indian mulatto boy, named ISRAEL TOLMEN, whose father was a white man, and mother an Indian; by profession a chimney-sweeper, and about nineteen years of age, five feet nine or ten inches high, hallow face, and very slender made, black short hair hangs about his neck, with brown eyes. Had on when he went away, an old calico coat, corduroy breeches, old hat and shoes; and it is expected he will change his cloaths.—He formerly lived with Col. Ray, and Mr. Samuel Turman, at Monmouth in Jersey, and is capable of telling a good tale, and has travelled much through the Jersey, and was born in Allen Town. Whoever takes up said runaway, and secures him in any gaol, so that his master gets him again, shall receive the above reward, and reasonable charges.
RICHARD ALLEN.

Philadelphia, Sept. 12, 1791.

N. B. All masters of vessels and others, are forbid harbouring or employing him at their peril.

In 1791, Richard Allen offered a "Four Dollars Reward" for the return of his runaway slave Israel Tolmen in this ironically named *Freeman's Journal* ad. *Newspapers.com.*

The ad was placed by Richard Allen, who added "N.B. All masters of vessels and others, are forbid harboring or employing him at their peril."

Who was the white father of Israel Tolmen, born around 1772? We know that slaves of the period were frequently given the family names of their owners, yet no standard Monmouth County reference work shows a Tolmen family. Notice that Israel had lived with "Mr. Samuel Turman," another unrecorded local family name. Spelling in newspapers of the time was notoriously capricious, but David Rhea did have a first cousin named Samuel Forman (1738–1817).

Samuel Forman married Margaret Forman in January 1772, around the same time his mulatto slave Israel was born. If Samuel Forman had impregnated an Indian slave, the child might have been light skinned and would likely resemble his father. Let's engage in some social speculations.

The twenty-one-year-old new bride, Margaret Forman, would be embarrassed, at the very least, by the presence of a baby who looked like her husband, especially since the child was not hers. Samuel Forman would have anticipated this awkward situation and would have given or sold the slave baby, Israel, to his cousin and friend David Rhea. In turn, David Rhea could realize a profit by selling Israel to Richard Allen sometime later, especially after the boy developed the unique and valuable skills of a chimney sweep.

Samuel Forman's will, written in 1806, mentions several slaves, among them "the negro girl named Terry…the boy named Joe…the boy named Tom" and, notably, "my *aged* slave named Dinah." Might Dinah have been a Native American, the "Indian" who gave birth to Israel thirty-four years before? It's certainly possible.

What would Israel's life have been like? Born into slavery and quickly sold and separated from his enslaved mother and a white father he never knew, his story was not uncommon in eighteenth-century New Jersey. He did not have Black parentage and grew up looking more like a white man. Whatever his countenance, Israel did not look like slaves of African descent and would be noticeably different from his mother's people, who were probably Lenapes.

Like every slave, Israel Tolmen/Forman hoped to escape bondage. He was an outsider by birth, by heritage and by the cruel enslavement wherein he was sold multiple times during the first two decades of his life. His work brought him into contact with many white people as he cleaned their chimneys. Maybe he found a family sympathetic to his situation, a family who provided temporary shelter and who had the wherewithal to help him escape.

Like so many of these runaway slave ads, there is no recorded follow-up indicating that Israel was found and returned to Richard Allen or if he completed a successful escape. Maybe he made his way north to New York and then to Canada. We'll never know.

***

I'm an old man now, I can't do nothing.
Young folks don't pay me no mind.
But in my day, I sure was something,
Before I felt the heavy hand of time.
—*Chris Stapleton, "Where Rainbows Never Die"*

The road to freedom is perilous, but few navigated it as successfully as the Reeves family. What Charles and Hannah Reeves accomplished in their long lives is all the more remarkable because they were both born enslaved in early nineteenth-century Middletown. Their resolute example inspired four generations of their descendants.

The hardships and triumphs of the Reeves family were preserved through the diligent research conducted by their great-granddaughter, the

Mae Edwards (*left*) researched her Reeves family history for years. She is pictured here with Muriel Roberts of the Afro-American Historical and Genealogical Society. *Rick Geffken.*

late Amanda Mae (Smack) Edwards. Mae died at eighty-six years old in 2019. She spent many years researching her African American ancestry. She accumulated hundreds of documents, photos and family stories. Mae traveled widely in pursuit of her family's roots. She became president of the Afro-American Historical and Genealogical Society New Jersey chapter, serving from 2008 to 2012.

For almost forty years, until her retirement in 1999, Mae Edwards was a medical surgical nurse at Riverview Hospital in Red Bank. She and her husband, Dock Edwards Jr., raised three children mere miles from her great-grandparents' humble beginnings in Middletown. Mae's prodigious memory and careful ancestral investigations provided the following details of the lives of Charles and Hannah Reeves.

The few written biographical details about Charles Reeves come from his September 1900 obituary: "Mr. Reeves was born at Holmdel [in May 1823]. In his youth he was a slave and was owned by David Williamson.

He was freed when he reached the age of twenty-five." Although no record of Reeves's slave birth or any Reeves/Williamson manumission documents exist in Monmouth County archives records, strong family tradition is important in this regard.

New Jersey tried for years to find a position between abolitionists and those who believed slavery was moral and necessary. Trenton legislators passed laws trying to appease both sides of this debate and thereby failed both. For instance, reacting to the tensions between East and West Jersey in March 1798, the state government passed an act that was dispiriting to both enslaved people and their abolitionist allies. It began with this statement: "That every negro, indian, mulatto or mestee, within this state, who, at the time of passing this act, is a slave for his or her life, shall continue such during his or her life; unless he or she, shall be manumitted and set free in the manner prescribed by law."

Half a dozen years later, the New Jersey Act for the Gradual Abolition of Slavery of 1804, although a progressive-sounding step, mandated that male African American slaves born after July 4 would remain "servants" until they reached twenty-five years of age, and women were required "to serve" until they were twenty-one. The law was only an abolition of slavery if you discounted the first two decades of a person's life. It was another pathetic attempt to right the historic wrong of slavery while simultaneously protecting the property of slaveholders.

Charles Reeves married Hannah B. Van Cleif in April 1850 at the Holmdel Baptist Church. No documents have been found that verify Hannah was born a slave or free or describing her status at the time of her marriage to Charles. Since absence of evidence is not evidence of absence, we rely on Mae Edwards's extensive research into her ancestry for the following biographical details of her forebears.

In the only known photograph of Charles Reeves, he poses elegantly late in his life, suggesting a proud Black man of regal bearing. Based on Charles's appearance in this picture, Mae Edwards believed that he might have had Native American ancestry. It was not unusual for Black people and Lenape Indians to marry when both marginalized groups were struggling to survive. Lenapes were enslaved alongside Africans from New Jersey's earliest days. Phrases like "negro, Indian and mulatto slaves" appear frequently in early newspaper ads, laws and statutes. For example, the New Jersey Supreme Court said in 1797, "They [the Indians] have been so long recognized as slaves in our law, that it would be as great a violation of the rights of property to establish a contrary doctrine at the present day, as it would be in the case of Africans."

The descendants of Charles Reeves believe he was born in Middletown, enslaved to David Williamson. *Amanda Mae (Smack) Edwards.*

Mrs. Claire Garland of Lincroft has documented the intermarriages in her own family of mixed heritage. Intriguingly, some of Garland's ancestors were named Reevey, perhaps an alternative spelling to Reeves. To date, any connection between the two families remains speculative, awaiting documentary verification.

Regarding Charles Reeves's ancestry, no Monmouth County white slaveholders named Reeves were found. Perhaps his family migrated from elsewhere. Descendants of a seventeenth-century white Reeves family migrated from Southampton, Long Island, to New Jersey, and one fought at the Battle of Monmouth in 1778. Though no direct linkage has been established, intriguingly, several of these white Long Island Reeveses were slaveholders.

Charles Reeves was emancipated from David Williamson around 1848. Williamson's brick house still stands on Newman Springs Road (in Middletown then and Holmdel today). Though in the first half of nineteenth century slaveholding was declining in Monmouth County, farmers like David Williamson still depended on slave labor, a way of life for generations in his family.

David Williamson married Phebe Hendrickson in 1834. She, too, was part of a long-established slaveholding family. Phebe's father, Daniel, owned three slaves, and her grandfather, Garrett Hendrickse Hendrickson, owned four slaves. Garrett Hendrickson's home, purchased from his cousin William Holmes in 1754, is also extant in Holmdel. (Now owned by the Monmouth County Park System, it's called the Holmes-Hendrickson House.) Where there were Hendricksons, there were slaves; seventeen slaves were owned by six different Hendricksons on a 1771 list of Middletown slaveholders.

Though chattel slavery was legal in New Jersey, the actual practice of enslavement was institutionalized in other ways as well. Many multigenerational slaveholding families in Monmouth County created their own traditions of human bondage through the simple and expedient method of bequeathing their enslaved people to their descendants via their last wills and testaments.

Garrett Hendrickson was among the signatories on a petition of February 1774 opposing the manumission of slaves. He needed bondsmen to work his large Pleasant Valley farm and to take care of the twelve children he had with three wives over his lifetime. The signers of that petition, with no apparent irony, included an appeal "to preserve the liberty of white people in this province." Any law freeing their slaves, they wrote, would "bring us into bondage which when once done would be very difficult to get rid of." Their arrogance still shocks today.

Left: Middletown's David Williamson owned a large farm, supported by slaves. This was his house as it appeared in 1851. *Jesse Lightfoot map, 1851.*

Below: The Holmes-Hendrickson House and farm in Pleasant Valley (Holmdel), built in the 1750s, depended on slave labor. *Monmouth County Historical Association.*

RES. OF DAVID WILLIAMSON
Holmdel.

Garrett Hendrickson died in 1801. The inventory of his property listed seven enslaved people. The men were named Peter and Tom; the woman was Jane; the boys were Peter, Jack and Robbin; and the girl was Pheby. We don't know how these people were related to one another. Their total listed value was £367, equivalent to more than $32,000 today.

As to Charles Reeves, we don't know if he moved away from David Williamson's farm immediately after gaining his freedom. Would he want to linger on his former owner's property with its ugly reminders of his forced labors? It's more likely that he would leave as soon as he found paid work somewhere else.

Hannah Van Cleif was also born in Middletown. Several historic documents list enslaved people with a Dutch last name like hers, indicating that Hannah or an ancestor were once owned by Van Cleifs (sometimes spelled Van Cleaf or Van Cleve). Different sources give her birth year as 1822 or 1830. This was not uncommon, since slaves often did not know their actual birth dates.

It's unclear which white family owned Hannah, although the Taylor family of Middletown had at least two slaves named Van Cleaf at their Kings Highway property. Three Taylors owned six slaves on the 1771 list; another list from 1798 has four Taylors owning thirteen slaves and notes "a tax of fifty cents was assessed upon each slave." It's possible, though not documented, that either William Van Cleaf (born in 1804) or his sister Elizabeth (1806) was a parent of Hannah or otherwise related to her.

Intriguingly, a Freehold blacksmith named William H. Bennett filed this Monmouth County record: "My said Negro woman named Sally Vancleaf had another female child born on the 21st day of June in the year of our Lord 1822 and called her name Hannah."

These fragmentary and sometimes conflicting records are another indication of how slaves were viewed—hardly consequential enough as human beings to record details of their lives. They were, we must constantly remind ourselves, viewed as property, interchangeable and always replaceable.

Speculations about Hannah's origins might be validated if a Williamson/Taylor nexus could be proved. The families do not appear to be related by blood but certainly would have known each other as contemporary Middletown slaveholders and people of wealth. Taylors and Hendricksons (the in-laws of David Williamson) appear on both lists of late eighteenth-century Middletown slaveholders.

Hannah Van Cleif was married to Charles Reeves in April 1850 by the Reverend William J. Nice, who performed the ceremony at the Holmdel Baptist Church (the little village once called Baptisttown). Hannah Van Cleif might have still been enslaved at the time of her wedding. If she was born in 1830, then she would not be eligible for emancipation until 1851.

A Reeves family Bible inscription shows that Hannah had a son five years before the wedding. She would have been only fifteen when Isaiah was born. Though early motherhood, or bearing children out of wedlock, was not unusual for enslaved women, Isaiah's listing is noticeably different from that of his subsequent siblings. John Smack, two-times great-grandson

Charles Reeves and Hannah Van Cleif were married at the Holmdel Baptist Church in April 1850. *John Smack.*

of Charles and Hannah Reeves, preserves that Reeves family Bible at his Navesink, New Jersey home today. Ten of the eleven Reeves children inscribed are specifically named as sons or daughters of both Charles and Hannah. The one exception is this: "Isaiah, son of Hannah Van Cleaf was born November the 5th 1845."

Charles Reeves was a free man on his wedding day, but her birth date of 1830 means that Hannah would have had to wait another ten months before attaining her freedom. So, if both adults were still enslaved when Isaiah was born, the child himself would have been born enslaved.

There is a gap of six years before Hannah had her second child, and the next nine children came along roughly every two to three years. Would the couple have waited six years between their first and second children? This suggests that Isaiah's father was not Charles Reeves. Charles might not have even known Hannah in 1845. Further, this opens the door to the possibility that Isaiah might have been fathered by Hannah's owner, whoever he was, an all too common occurrence at the time.

Mae Edwards was not able to discover how her great-grandparents Charles and Hannah met. They might have been owned by the same family or possibly worked for neighboring families. They might have been a loving couple before they married, and Isaiah was their "illegitimate" son. Regardless, Isaiah was raised alongside the other children and always identified as a Reeves.

As to the status of the Reeveses at their marriage, it's possible that Hannah's owner, whomever he was, released her from bondage earlier than the law required, perhaps as a wedding present. Or perhaps he simply saw her marriage as a chance to relieve himself of the upkeep of Hannah and her baby—and maybe even Charles, too, if they were all owned by the same family. Then again, their owner could have manumitted the entire new family when Isaiah was born. No records exist to solve this mystery.

John Smack says:

> *I'm of the belief that Charles was not [Isaiah's] father. They both seem very religious and would probably not have engaged in any [intimate] activity prior to getting married. Also, I believe whoever wrote in the Bible would have mentioned that he was Charles's son born out of wedlock, as whoever was writing this seemed to know the importance of history. Someone else, most likely the slave owner, fathered Isaiah. Charles and Hannah were born during a transition. They were definitely born into slavery because they were children of slaves. The transition was that they did not have to serve their entire lives as slaves but almost enjoyed, for lack of a better word, the benefits of "indenturement," which gave them a limited number of years that they would have to serve.*

The last child born to Charles and Hannah Reeves was Amanda. She and nine of her ten siblings survived into the twentieth century. Amanda married John Norman in 1895. Maude E. Norman was born half a dozen years after Charles Reeves died, but her grandmother, Hannah, lived another eighteen years after Charles's death. With her parents, Maude lived in Hannah's home until she was twelve.

Maude Norman knew most of her aunts and uncles who were born between 1851 and 1872. Maude shared the family history with her daughter, Mae. Preserving family lore was easy because Maude and Mae were always reminded of the lives and times of their ancestors; they grew up in the very same house. It was located on Middletown-Lincroft Road and was home to four consecutive generations. It is a crucial part of the Reeves family story.

Around the turn of the twentieth century, a journalist named Katherine Prence traveled through Middletown by horse and buggy. A faded brown copy of the newspaper article she wrote has been passed down to John Smack. In it, Prence described her impressions as she left Lincroft:

> *And turning off due north towards Middletown village and bay. A negro's cabin, dotted down by the wayside, pleasantly harmonized with the general tone of the scene. Its gray and weather-beaten front, guiltless of paint this many a year, was sheathed, even to the attic windows, in a tangled mass of wisteria. A leafless poplar traced its thin, vertical silhouette against that wall of green; and by the doorway, in the sunshine, a broad-faced old turbaned mammy sat serenely knitting. Marigolds, struggling together tumultuously in an unkept bed, flared into the picture with their strong orange light. A faded quilt of many colors swung from a line nearby; and, as a last touch of warmth and homeliness, the little dome-like apple tree that hugged the eaves so closely was studded to its last capacity with bright red balls of fruit.*

This intimate portrait—Prence was clearly captivated by the old woman on her front porch—is a description of Hannah Reeves sitting on her porch

Around 1900, Hannah Reeves posed for this photograph at her house on Middletown-Lincroft Road. *John Smack.*

on a late summer day. How the Reeves family came to live in that home is a unique post-slavery story.

Shortly after his marriage in 1850, the freeman Charles Reeves was working on the farm of Garrett D. Hendrickson, a cousin of Reeves's former owner David Williamson's wife, Phebe. By 1870, after Garrett Hendrickson's death, Reeves was employed by George W. Crawford of the Nut Swamp section of Middletown. Charles stayed with Crawford for the rest of his life. The Reeves house originally stood on Crawford's Lincroft farm.

The Reeves family story is that George Crawford liked Charles Reeves so much that he "gave" him the house and a small piece of property. Maude Norman recalled it this way in 1972: "My grandmother, Hannah Van Cleif Reeves once remarked [to George W. Crawford] how she'd love to live in that house. At the time it was located on a brook on the grounds of what is now Christian Brothers Academy. Mr. Crawford had the house moved to where it sits now, and, after my grandfather had worked for him for twenty years, he gave him the house and a burial plot behind St. Leo's School."

Documentary evidence adheres closely to the Reeves family story. A note in the family Bible says that the house was built in 1836 on Crawford property. More a rudimentary shack than a substantial dwelling, it might have been slave quarters originally. It was moved, probably on rolling logs, to a lot next to a stream on the east side of Middletown-Lincroft Road sometime around 1863.

The house, however, was not an outright gift from Crawford. An 1889 map of Lincroft, when it was still called Leedsville, shows that George Crawford owned the property. A deed written just three months before Charles died in 1900 indicates that George Crawford's son James sold the property to James Reeves, son of Charles. This suggests that George Crawford and Charles Reeves had an agreement in which the formerly enslaved man and his family were allowed to live in the home while Reeves worked for Crawford. These kinds of deals were known as "cottaging."

Whether George Crawford's extraordinary gesture came from guilt, Christian charity or simply earnest goodwill, we can't say, but his generosity helped change the course of the lives of the Reeves family, outdone only by Charles and Hannah's own kindness, persistence and industry.

The Reeveses no doubt grew subsistence crops on their half acre of land, but they'd have had a difficult time feeding a large family from a backyard garden alone. With thirteen people under his roof, Reeves also needed a salary from Crawford. In effect, Reeves was indentured, contracted to work

N. J. WARRANTY DEED.—151.

CHISHOLM, DAVIS & CO., 20 WARREN STREET, N. Y.

This Indenture,

Made the *Thirty first* day of *May* , in the year of our Lord One Thousand Nine Hundred

Between JAMES F. CRAWFORD (unmarried)

of the Township of Middletown in the County of Monmouth and State of New Jersey, party of the first part;

And

JAMES REEVES, son of Charles and Hannah Reeves

of the Township of Middletown in the County of Monmouth and State of New Jersey, party of the second part:

Witnesseth, That the said party of the first part, for and in consideration of ONE DOLLAR (and other good and valuable considerations)

lawful money of the United States of America, to him in hand well and truly paid by the said party of the second part, at or before the sealing and delivery of these presents, the receipt whereof is hereby acknowledged, and the said party of the first part being therewith fully satisfied, contented and paid, has given, granted, bargained, sold, aliened, released, enfeoffed, conveyed and confirmed, and by these presents do es give, grant, bargain, sell, alien, release enfeoff, convey and confirm unto the said party of the second part, and to his heirs and assigns, forever, **All** that tract or parcel of land and premises, hereinafter particularly described, situate, lying and being in the Township of Middletown in the County of Monmouth and State of New Jersey,

BEGINNING at a stake standing in the center of a brook and in line of Sarah Ann Slocum's land and from thence running as the magnetic Needle pointed Oct. 12, 1882 (1) north eighty seven degrees west three chains and forty eight links along said Slocum to the center of the public highway leadin g from Leedsville to Middletown

James Crawford sold the home and property where Charles Reeves and his family had lived for thirty years to a son, James Reeves, just before Charles died. *John Smack.*

off the value of his home and property for years before he could own it outright. This situation was in line with the intent of an 1846 New Jersey law "that every such person shall...become and be an apprentice, bound to service to his or her present owner...which service shall continue until such person is discharged therefrom, as is hereinafter directed." Four generations of Reeveses lived in that Lincroft home before it was sold in 1979 and then demolished to make way for a modern house.

Can you run
to the Freedom Line
of the Lincoln soldiers?
—Chris Stapleton, "Can You Run"

A long overlooked and overgrown little plot of land not too far from the Reeves home in Lincroft reveals how the Civil War touched Monmouth County in ways not often taught in local schools. In the now mostly upscale section of suburban Middletown, just off Hurleys Lane and adjacent to St. Leo the Great's Roman Catholic Church, Cedar View Cemetery has remained hidden for 170 years. This small piece of property was sold to fourteen Black men by a white man in 1850. Interred within are over a dozen Black people—United States Colored Troops or USCTs—who fought for the freedom of thousands during our Civil War.

Another Crawford played a prominent role in the story of this cemetery. Graveyard researcher and historian Ed Raser notes, "On 14 November 1850, John B. Crawford [and his wife Catharine], a wealthy area farmer, and former slave owner, for $60, sold a 2.05-acre tract to fourteen black men 'to be used for a buying ground.'" John Crawford was the father of George, who employed Charles Reeves. Three of the cemetery buyers were the brothers Elijah, Jesse and Alexander Frost. The other men were Silas Reeves, Hosea Reeves, Joseph Reeves, Edward Shomo, Lloyd Johnson, Samuel Schanck, Jacob Wall, Francis Beldo, James Taylor, John Holmes and Samuel Kearney.

Ella Paoni, a modern-day fourth-generation resident of Lincroft, suggests that the Crawford sale was related to the Fugitive Slave Act of 1850. Congress passed it on September 18 as part of the Compromise of 1850. The act required that runaway slaves be returned to their owners,

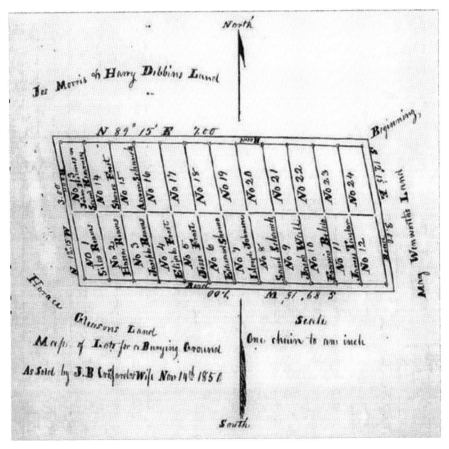

The two-acre Cedar View Cemetery plot (Lincroft) was purchased by fourteen free African American men from John B. Crawford in 1850. *Joseph A. Grabas.*

even if they escaped to a state that had abolished slavery. Anyone harboring runaways or refusing to help return them to their rightful owners was liable for substantial fines.

Sensing easy financial opportunity, unscrupulous slave catchers seeking quick rewards kidnapped Black people at random—slave or free—and sent them to southern states. New Jersey shamefully gave official sanction to the forced return of fugitive slaves. Historian James Gigantino wrote that New Jersey politicians consistently communicated "solidarity with southerners, a desire for law and order on the border." Another historian, Beverly C. Tomek, added to Gigantino's argument, writing, "A significant number of New Jersey citizens saw the fugitives, rather than the slave catchers, as the source of disruption and lawlessness."

So, although there were only a few hundred slaves left in New Jersey by 1850, perhaps the fourteen Black purchasers of the Lincroft cemetery still felt at risk of capture. Note that the two acres were deeded just a month after the act was passed. The buyers might have appealed to an already sympathetic John Crawford with a plea that a deed would be verifiable proof that they were free New Jersey property owners and therefore protected from kidnapping.

Twenty years later, Alexander Frost sold a portion (No. 12) of his cemetery plot to Charles Reeves for ten dollars. The ninety-nine-by-thirty-eight-foot plot contains the remains of at least a dozen Reeves descendants, each one marked with a stone, unlike any of the other thirteen plots.

Cedar View Cemetery is an anomaly—one of a few Monmouth County cemeteries entirely owned by Black people during the mid-nineteenth century. No one knows the exact number of souls buried there. Rob Shomo, formerly of Seabright, New Jersey, and now living in North Carolina, has done extensive research on the people interred in Cedar View. Several of his ancestors are buried there, including USCT Silas Reeves (no known relation to Charles Reeves). Silas Reeves's grave marker is in the very front of the cemetery, which might be why, for many years, the burial ground was alternately called the Reeves Cemetery.

New Jersey military historian Joseph G. Bilby has noted, "Of the tens of thousands of New Jerseyans who served in the Union Army, only 900 were draftees. Beginning in 1863, African-Americans flocked to the Union ranks as well." At the outbreak of the Civil War in 1861, Charles and Hannah Reeves had six children; another would be born during the war years. As sympathetic to the Union cause as the Reeveses surely were, we have no indication that the hardworking family man, nor any of his sons, served during the conflict fought over slavery.

Almost inevitably, the burial ground was forgotten over time. It lay neglected for decades, under constant threat of development for housing lots. A teenaged Edwin Edwards accompanied his mother, Mae, in 1991 in the first effort to identify relatives buried at the cemetery and to clean up their gravesites. As this book goes to press, a Friends of Cedar View Cemetery is working to restore the hallowed grounds and to attain its overdue historic recognition.

Late in their lives, Charles and Hannah Reeves would walk from their Lincroft home for three miles along West Front Street to a little Baptist house of worship on Water Street in Red Bank. After spending morning services in prayer and observance, the couple would walk back home. Sometimes,

Charles Reeves Jr. put black granite markers on the graves of his parents, Hannah and Charles Reeves. *Rick Geffken*.

Charles would return to church the same evening. Eventually, the couple rode to church together on a single horse, and when they could finally afford it, they took their children to church by horse and wagon. The Reeveses were among the original congregants of what is now the Pilgrim Baptist Church community on Shrewsbury Avenue in Red Bank. Charles Reeves's 1900 *Red Bank Register* obituary read, "Mr. Reeves was one of the best-known colored men in Middletown township. He was a member of the Baptist church at Red Bank, and for thirty-three years had rarely missed a Sunday."

Another story in a privately published little book about Lincroft speaks to the generous spirit of Hannah Reeves. During heavy snowstorms, two groups of men would work their way toward each another while shoveling along Middletown-Lincroft Road. "They always managed to meet in front of the home of Miss Hannah Van Cleef Reeves. 'Aunt Hannah' as she was affectionately called, invited them into her kitchen where she had ready for them hot tea or cocoa and a home-made cake."

Hannah Reeves lived another two decades before she died in 1918. The couple rest side by side beneath matching black granite stones in the little Cedar View Cemetery. Engraved with just their names and dates, the markers were lovingly carved and put in place years later by their son Charles Reeves Jr., who worked for a monument company in West Long Branch.

5

MIDDLESEX COUNTY

SLAVE ENTREPÔT

There are strange things happening every day.
If you want to view the climb
You must learn to quit your lyin'.
There are strange things happening every day.
—"Strange Things Happening Every Day,"
traditional African American spiritual

Middlesex County's connections to slavery date to its earliest days. After the English took over from the Dutch in 1664, James Stuart, Duke of York and the brother of King Charles II, gave two of his associates the vast territory that became New Jersey. Stuart was president and principal stockholder of the Royal African Company, chartered in 1660 to trade in gold, silver, timber and Africans. Among the company's steering committee members was Sir George Carteret.

A stock offering from what was first called the Company of Royal Adventurers Trading into Africa read, matter-of-factly, "The Royal Company being very sensible how necessary it is that the English Plantations in America should have a competent and a constant supply of Negro-servants for their own use of Planting…shall within eight days dispatch so many Ships for the Coast of Africa as shall by God's permission furnish the said Plantations with at least 3000 Negroes." (This invocation of God ignored the brutal inhumanity of the enterprise and recalls Hannah Arendt's famous "banality of evil" description of another infamous atrocity three centuries later.)

James, Duke of York, was president of the Royal African Company, which was chartered in 1660 to trade in gold, silver, timber and African people for the American colonies. *Museum of London.*

The company's slave ships landed at Perth Amboy, the major slave port in New Jersey, and at other unguarded and remote locations along the Jersey coast—a way to avoid tariffs imposed at the Port of New York. Reports indicate that these captured African men and women had their chests branded with the company's acronym, RAC.

Lord John Berkeley and Sir George Carteret were the two men favored with the land grant from James Stuart. The pair issued the founding document of our state, *The Concession and Agreement of the Lords Proprietors of the Province of New Caesarea.* To ensure "that the planting of the said province may be the more speedily promoted," the *Concession* offered prospective colonists seventy-five acres of land "for every weaker servant, or slave, male or female" brought with them. After this initial incentive, yearly acreage per slave decreased to forty-five acres and then to thirty acres. Thus slavery was established and entrenched in New Jersey for the next two centuries.

In August 1702, Queen Anne of England issued instructions to her cousin Edward Hyde, Lord Cornbury, when she appointed him as royal governor of New York and New Jersey. She admonished him to make certain nothing interfered with the trafficking of slaves in the province. He was encouraged to assist the Royal African Company's existing efforts at the slave port of Perth Amboy, so "the said province should have a constant and sufficient supply of merchantable negroes at moderate rates in money or commodities… and you are yearly to give unto us, and to our commissioners for trade and plantations, an account of what number of Negroes our said province is yearly supplied with, and at what rates."

Perth Amboy was the principal East Jersey entrepôt for slaves, as was Cooper's Ferry (Camden) in West Jersey. Imported slaves were kept chained in a barracks until they could be auctioned off and redistributed throughout the Jerseys and New York to satisfy the growing demand for cheap agricultural labor.

Recalling his youth in Perth Amboy, William Dunlap, born in 1766, wrote:

> *Holding negroes in slavery was in those days the common practice, and the voices of those who protested against the evil were not heard. Every house in my native place where any servants were to be seen, swarmed with black slaves—every house save one, hereafter to be mentioned. My father's kitchen had several families of them of all ages, and all born in the family of my mother except one, who was called a new-negro, and had his face tattooed....These blacks indulged me of course, and I sought the kitchen as the place where I found playmates...and the place where I found amusement to, and forming my taste, in the mirth and games of the negroes, and the variety of visiters [sic] of the black race who frequented the place.*

The adult Dunlap recognized, atypically, how corrupting slavery was for many in New Jersey society as he continued, "This may be considered my first school....Such is the school of many a one even now....The infant is taught to tyrannize—the boy is taught to despise labor—the mind of the child is contaminated by hearing and seeing which perhaps is not understood at the time, but remains with the memory."

———•———

AFTER THE AMERICAN REVOLUTION, Thomas Jefferson held contradictory and confounding attitudes toward slavery. The founding father who enshrined "all men are created equal" in our Declaration of Independence owned hundreds of slaves who worked at his Monticello plantation in Virginia. Jefferson also lived with, and had children by, his deceased wife's half-sister, his slave Sally Hemings.

And yet, as our young country expanded westward across the Appalachians just after the Revolutionary War, this same Thomas Jefferson proposed banning the introduction of slavery into any new incorporated territories. Remarkably, it was an action, or rather an inaction, of a New Jersey man that prevented Jefferson's hope that slavery wouldn't spread to future states.

Had this Princeton man voted to support Jefferson's proposal in 1784, the Civil War might not have occurred seventy-seven years later.

Here's the backstory. Before George Washington, another slaveholder, became our first president in 1789, the Congress of Confederation was responsible for the legislative and executive functions of the fledgling government. Congressional delegates met in a series of locations, including New York City, Philadelphia, Princeton and Trenton. These became temporary de facto capitals of the county while Congress conducted its business, debated the founding principles and wrote our founding documents.

Congress met in the Maryland State House in Annapolis for most of 1784. In March, Thomas Jefferson wrote and submitted a five-part proposal addressing his vision of western expansion. Article five of this proposal read, "That after the year 1800 of the Christian era, there shall be neither slavery nor involuntary servitude in any of the said States." Jefferson, an astute politician, was convinced that he had the requisite number of votes for his proposal to be adopted into law.

Each of the new states was represented by two Confederation Congressional delegates in 1784. Dr. John Beatty was one of the New Jersey delegates. (The other was William C. Houston of Somerset County.) Beatty, born in Pennsylvania, had graduated from the College of New Jersey (now Princeton University) in 1769. He became a medical doctor, served in the Continental army during the Revolutionary War, was captured by the British and then was exchanged for other prisoners. After the war, he was a permanent resident of Middlesex County, serving as a member of its legislative council from 1781 to 1783.

JOHN BEATTY, M.D.
Member of the Continental Congress.

Dr. John Beatty was the Continental Congress delegate who missed a crucial vote on slavery in 1784. *Library of Congress.*

Thomas Jefferson wrote a letter to another future president, James Madison, on April 25, 1784. In it, Jefferson described the day his ordinance banning slavery came up for vote: "You will observe two clauses struck out of the report, the first respecting hereditary honours, the second slavery....The second was lost by an individual vote only. Ten states were present. The four Eastern states, New York, [and] Pennsylvania were for the clause. Jersey would have been for it, but there were but two members, one of whom was sick in his chambers. Thus, we see the fate of millions unborn hanging on the tongue of one man, and heaven was silent in that awful moment."

New Jersey's Dr. John Beatty was the delegate too ill to vote on that fateful day. The National Archives website offers this rueful explanation: "The Ordinance of 1784 passed without the slavery provision on April 23, 1784. Every delegate including and north of Pennsylvania voted for Thomas Jefferson's clause excluding slavery; Jefferson and [Hugh] Williamson (North Carolina) were the only delegates southward of that state to vote with them. The lack of the vote of a single delegate determined the outcome."

What if John Beatty had voted on that April day for Jefferson's proposal to stop the westward expansion of slavery in the United States? Would the abolition of slavery have happened sooner? Would the Civil War have occurred?

A few years after the failed vote, a healed and hopeful Jefferson revisited the issue: "The voice of a single individual would have prevented this abominable crime; heaven will not always be silent; the friends to the rights of human nature will in the end prevail." As it happened, Jefferson was prescient, but it would take an extremely bloody conflict between the states before those "rights of human nature" were settled into law.

OCCASIONALLY, AND RARELY, NEW JERSEY showed gratitude for slaves who had served during the Revolutionary War. In September 1784, *An Act for Setting Free Peter Williams, A Negro, Late the Property of John Heard* was passed by the New Jersey Legislature. Heard took his slave Williams with him to serve under the British. But Williams left to join the Continental army, "where he served faithfully until the End of the War." When Heard's Woodbridge estate was confiscated, Williams became state property.

In recognition of his patriotic service, the legislature declared Peter Williams "to be manumitted and set free from Slavery and Servitude, as fully to all Intents and Purposes as though he had been free born and continued in such a State of Freedom; *any Law, Usage, or Custom to the contrary notwithstanding.*"

In April 1787, a widow named Catherine Burlew, who lived in Cheesequake (Old Bridge Township), sold a "Negrow slave Named Dick" to James Provoost for £100, more than $16,000 in today's money. Both principals resided in the same Raritan Bay town, and their families knew each other well. Provoost gave Burlew a £34 down payment and his bond for the balance. The twenty-five-year-old Provoost was newly married, and Dick would be a valuable addition to his accumulation of wealth.

But James Provoost died in 1790, leaving his wife, Anna (Bowne), to pay off the balance of the debt, with interest, over the next four years. This was yet another transaction where slaves were devalued as human beings while being valued simply as trade goods.

The Burlew family (shortened from the original Buckelew) had settled in Middlesex County in the late seventeenth century. Samuel Obadiah Burlew married Catherine Gerrit Covenhoven of Freehold in January 1775. Samuel was once a private in Captain James Morgan's company of the Middlesex County Militia during the Revolutionary War. At the end of that conflict, Samuel Burlew settled into farming, using slaves to help work his land.

Ten years into their marriage, Burlew died at thirty-five years old. His widow, Catherine, was left to care for a daughter and a son, both under nine years old. The prospect must have been daunting for a single parent who needed income. Her most obvious disposable asset was the slave, Dick. She sold him less than two years after the death of her husband. We don't know how Dick became enslaved to the Burlews. It is possible that he was a

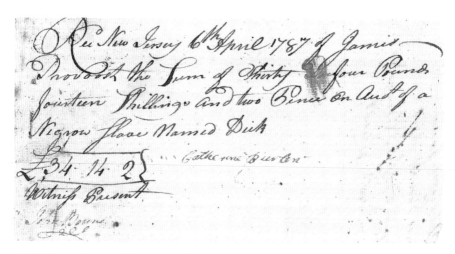

A Middlesex County widow named Catherine Burlew sold her slave Dick in April 1787. *Bob Schoeffling.*

104

wedding gift from Catherine's father, Gerret Covenhoven, who bequeathed several slaves to his children. The Covenhovens were a Dutch family of slaveholding farmers in Marlboro.

As is so often the case with eighteenth-century slaves, we know little about Dick, save for a few scant records concerning his sale. Performing backbreaking farm labor, did he also endure punishments meted out for disobedience or perceived incompetence? Did he marry, have children or suffer the hardships of being separated from his family? Did he remain in New Jersey, or was he sold again and sent to parts unknown? Where is he buried? There is no further mention of Dick, nor any recording of his manumission. But for the survival of a few receipts on slim pieces of withering paper, the man named Dick would be totally anonymous.

Anna Bowne Provoost doesn't seem to have struggled much financially after her husband, James's, death. He left her and their two small children a substantial estate worth £642. (This was such a substantial estate that her family suspected her subsequent marriage to Dr. Aaron Pitney four years later was less about love than his gold digging.) Nonetheless, and to illustrate how disposable slaves were to people in late eighteenth-century New Jersey, the well-off widow Provoost sold another of her slaves.

Several notations in an old book of James Provoost's receipts (owned now by Monmouth County historical commissioner Peter VanNortwick) indicate that Anna Provoost sold the slave Jube to William Hillyer in 1792. Because Jube fetched less than half of Dick's sale price—only forty pounds—he was probably older and therefore thought to be worth less. Hillyer paid for Jube with four installments over a year.

Hillyer was connected to the Burlew and Bowne families through marriage. His wife was Mary Burlew, a first cousin of Samuel Burlew. As an ensign (an army rank then), Hillyer was wounded at the Battle of Monmouth in June 1778, when he, too, served under Captain James Morgan.

Thus Captain Morgan is the nexus between many of these people. Samuel Burlew and William Hillyer both served during the Revolution in Morgan's New Jersey Militia. Among his other military assignments, Morgan commanded the guards at Cheesequake. He was captured with his son Jamy by the British, but James Sr. evaded imprisonment. Jamy Morgan did time in the notorious Sugar House jail in New York. Captain Morgan was something of a slavecatcher, albeit a semisuccessful one.

During March 1778, as the Revolutionary War raged, Captain Morgan took possession of two Negro "fellows," slaves who ran away from their owners in Staten Island and made it to South Amboy when Morgan was

A slave named Jeb (or Jube) was sold by William Hillyer in 1793 for forty pounds sterling. *Peter VanNortwick.*

stationed there. He advertised for their rightful owners in the *New Jersey Gazette*. Joe was twenty-six, and Hack was about sixty years old. Both were tall, around six feet. Morgan hoped for a reward and reimbursement for his troubles taking care of the valuable pair. We don't know if Morgan was rewarded, though it's probable.

A few years later, in 1781, Morgan was at it again, placing an ad in the *Philadelphia Gazette* noting that he had captured a runaway "Mulattoe Slave" named Will. This slave had escaped from a Benjamin Bunker at New Castle, Delaware. Will was twenty-four years old, five foot, nine inches tall, and "ties his wool behind," the last description a derogatory reference to Will's hair. Will was apparently making his way to New York when Morgan caught him. Subsequently, Will escaped again by swimming across Cheesequake Creek. Will was trying to get to Staten Island, a short row in a stolen boat across Raritan Bay. We have no information on the final disposition of these captured runaways, though it's a fair guess that they were taken back to their owners and punished severely.

The Morgan most notorious for his slavery misdeeds is another of Captain James Morgan's sons, his youngest, Charles. Born around 1775, Charles was a baby during the War for Independence, but like the rest of his family, he grew up depriving other people of their personal freedom.

Fifty Hard Dollars Reward.

THE Mulattoe Slave, named WILL, that run away the 19th of August, 1781, from Benjamin Bunker, in New-Castle county, State of Delaware, was taken up by Captain James Morgan, living in South-Amboy, Middlesex county, East-Jersey, has got away from him; he is a smart well made fellow, about 24 years of age, 5 feet 9 inches high, marked with the small pox, and ties his wool behind; he lost his clothes in swimming across a creek, all but an old felt hat; he likes to play on the violin, and loves strong drink. He was raised by Capt. John Edwards, in the above county. Whoever takes up the said fellow, and secures him in any goal, so that his master may get him again, shall have the above reward, paid by

Nov. 6. † 7 w. BENJAMIN BUNKER.

Above: The runaway "Mulattoe Slave" Will escaped from Delaware and swam across Cheesequake Creek trying to get to Staten Island. Philadelphia Gazette *via Newspapers.com*.

Left: Charles Morgan was part of a notorious scheme to ship New Jersey African Americans into slavery in Louisiana. *Louisiana State University Library*.

For every hard earned dollar I make,
There stands a white man just to take it away.
Some might say I talk loud, see if I care.
Unlike them, don't walk away from my fear
I've busted bones, broken stones, looked the devil in the eye,
I hope he's going to break these chains, oh yeah.
—JJ Julius Son/KALEO, "Broken Bones"

An 1812 New Jersey law restricted the sale of slaves to another state without their consent. This ostensibly well-meaning attempt to reckon with the evils of slavery, together with the 1804 Act for the Gradual Abolition of Slavery, helped create a true black market. Slaves were worth more as commodities than their value as laborers. Slaves who were worth $300 in New Jersey were selling for almost $800 in New Orleans.

The largest markets for these enslaved people were in southern states bordering the Gulf of Mexico, places where "Cotton was King" and cheap (free) manual labor was becoming harder to attain. Southern newspapers lauded "Jersey negroes" as particularly well suited because of their agricultural skills. The *New Orleans Chronicle* wrote, "We are much indebted to the enterprising and successful exertions of Mr. Charles Morgan, for the copiousness of the present supply [of Jersey negroes] which…will probably suffice for the next crop."

Charles Morgan, son of Captain James, had moved from New Jersey to Louisiana. He owned a plantation called Morganza in Point Coupee Parish, on the Mississippi River just north of Baton Rouge. Styling himself Colonel Morgan, he decided slaves would make a handsome investment when he took a trip to his Middlesex County ancestral home in 1818. Charles and his brother-in-law Jacob Van Wickle (married to Sarah Morgan) partnered in an illegal moneymaking scheme to buy New Jersey slaves and then transport and sell them at profit in Louisiana. The illegality arose because the law required the consent of Black people, hardly something they would do. To make it worse, Van Wickle happened to be a Middlesex County judge with apparently few scruples when it came to enriching himself. He was also the uncle of Ann Van Wickle, wife of Jamy Morgan, Charles's brother.

Judge Van Wickle "interviewed" dozens of slaves and free Blacks and later represented that they consented to go to Louisiana of their own free

Judge Jacob Van Wickle held African Americans at his home while he "interviewed" them for their "consent" to be shipped to New Orleans. *Slaves Waiting for Sale, Richmond, Virginia by Eyre Crowe, 1861.*

will. He lied to them, promising they could make good wages in the South. The judge enlisted his son Nicholas to buy New Jersey slaves at the cheapest going rate. The judge lied again on manifest documents, purporting the legal transport of consenting slaves on two ships heading for Louisiana. To make these transactions appear legal, the good judge signed numerous phony consent forms, some of which he postdated, which allowed for the removal of Middlesex County slaves. One read:

> *Removal Harvey*
> *State of New Jersey*
> *Middlesex County*
> *Be it remembered on this twenty seventh day of February of our Lord one thousand eight hundred eighteen Nicholas Van Wickle of the county of Middlesex in New Jersey, brought before us Jacob Van Wickle and John Outcalt Esquires two of the judges of the court of Common Pleas of the county and State aforesaid, his male Slave named Harvey aged 14 years and the said Harvey having no parents in said state, being by us examined separate and apart from his said master declared that he was willing, and*

that he freely consented to remove and go out of this State to Point Coupee in the State of Louisiana and there to serve Colonel Charles Morgan and Nicholas Van Wickle or either of them, for the term of twenty five years three months & four days from the date hereof their heirs, executors, administrators and assigns jointly and severally.

In Testimony whereof we have heretofore set our hands the day and year first above written.

Jacob Van Wickle
John Outcalt
Judges

The declaration that Harvey was willing "to serve" Charles Morgan and Nicholas Van Wickle was itself fictitious—the two were only partners on paper. Nicholas Van Wickle had no intention of leaving New Jersey and never moved to Louisiana.

The brig *Mary Ann* left New York bound for New Orleans on March 10, 1818, with its cargo of thirty-nine slaves. The ship took on more human cargo, about thirty-six slaves, just off Sandy Hook during a rendezvous with the South Amboy packet sloop *Thorne*, captained by John D. Disbrow. Disbrow was still another Morgan in-law, married to Susannah, the daughter of Captain James Morgan.

Despite a United States Revenue Cutter search at the Hook, the *Thorne* was cleared to proceed carrying these deceived African Americans, in violation of existing transport law. With Charles Morgan aboard, the sloop returned to shore and loaded up another thirty-nine unsuspecting Black people at Perth Amboy, ironically the very port into which the Royal African Company first brought slaves to New Jersey in the seventeenth century. Fully loaded with unsuspecting Black New Jersey citizens, the *Thorne* set off for New Orleans. One of the Black women on board said she had lived with Judge Van Wickle and now wanted to live with "Massa Charles." If her statement wasn't coerced, she must have gone along with the subterfuge simply as a matter of survival.

The *Mary Ann* arrived in New Orleans on May 10, 1818. The people who disembarked were not on the manifest as specified by law. Surviving lists are incomplete or conflicting. The most common accounting suggests that their names were Susan; Peter; Moses; Harry; James; Bob; George; Simon; Susan Watt; Elmirah; Betsy; Bass; Lidia; Patty; Claresse and child Hercules; Rachel; Ann and child Regina; Flora and child Susan; Jeanette Lydia Ann and child Harriet; Jane; Hager and three children Rosinah,

UNITED STATES SLAVE TRADE.
1830.

Two ships, the *Thorne* and the *Mary Ann*, illegally transported Blacks from South Amboy to New Orleans, where they were sold into slavery. *Library of Congress.*

Mary and Augustus; Christeen and two children Diana and Dorcas; Margaret Coven; and Sarah and child Dianah. Several others might have died on the voyage south from New Jersey.

An incomplete list of the people who were landed from the *Thorne* shows that their names were Nancy, Joseph, James, John, Phillis, Charles, Gilda, Sam, Susan Silvey, Joe and Jude.

Morgan's scheme was discovered when Louisiana customs officials noticed discrepancies in the *Mary Ann*'s manifests. The ship's captain was brought to trial, but a sympathetic southern jury let him go. Charles Morgan was not off the legal hook quite yet, however. He and Nicholas Van Wickle were indicted in New Jersey. They made enough money in the scheme to hire expert and connected attorneys, and the pair evaded punishment. A few incidental players were convicted of minor offenses. Judge Van Wickle, the "mastermind" of the entire scheme, escaped legal consequences altogether.

What do we know about the fate of these New Jersey slaves who were shipped to Louisiana? Precious little, though some were undoubtedly forced to work at the Morganza plantation. Others of the displaced northerners might have been sold to other planters eager for "Jersey negroes."

It would be heartwarming to report that some of these tricked and enslaved people survived the Civil War and were freed by troops from their home state of New Jersey. Alas, that did not eventuate. The farthest south New Jersey troops fought was at the Battle of Mobile in Alabama.

Maybe the transported children, Hercules, Regina, Susan, Harriet, Rosinah, Mary, Augustus, Diana, Dorcas and Dianah, lived to hear of Lincoln's Emancipation Proclamation in 1863. Maybe when they were liberated following the Civil War, they found a better life during Reconstruction, before the harshness of Jim Crow beset them. Perhaps, on some slim chance, a few of those who'd been hoodwinked returned to their native New Jersey.

We do know that some of those kidnapped were sold to other Louisiana slaveholders. Their descendants survive today. One scholar's extensive research project reports that "some of the laborers brought to Petite Anse from New Jersey…founded major kinship groups with lines extending until 1860" and beyond. Recent DNA studies have also confirmed New Jersey heritage for a group of Black Louisianans.

ANOTHER BRANCH OF THE Morgan family participated in and perpetuated enslavement in New Jersey for as long as they possibly could. Nicholas Morgan Disbrow, son of John D. and Susannah Morgan Disbrow, was born in the Matchaponix section of Old Bridge on October 8, 1782. As we've seen, chattel slavery and the buying and selling of Black people were ordinary facets of the Morgan and Disbrow families for the better part of a century.

When Nicholas Disbrow was fifty-three years old, in 1835, he took out several weekly ads in the *Monmouth Democrat* newspaper of Freehold. Disbrow wanted to sell his slave Yaff (a fairly common slave name and no known connection to the Yaff discussed in chapter 2). This slave was apparently more of a problem to Disbrow than his worth. Yaff was in the Freehold jail, possibly having been captured by a Mr. J.M. Hartshorne. Yaff was forty-five years old and a constant runaway. Disbrow was tired of tracking him down again and again, not to mention the expenses involved in paying rewards for his retrieval.

A few years previously, the 1830 federal census listed Disbrow's household, consisting of eight white people and three "Free Colored Persons." These last were two men between twenty-four and thirty-six and a woman between ten and twenty-four, all unnamed. Why would Disbrow have both free and enslaved people in his household? One real possibility was that he listed some as free to avoid tax consequences of property he owned. That he was an attorney and a county judge was merely incidental.

SLAVE FOR SALE.

THE Subscriber will sell for a reasonable price, his SLAVE, named Yaff, aged about
45 years, and now confined in the Monmouth
Couty Goal.

For particulars, inquire of J. M. Hartshorne,
at Freehold, or the Subscriber at Middletown-
Point.   NICHOLAS M. DISBROW.

March 6th, 1835.   3w.

Keyport stagecoach business owner Nicholas Disbrow advertised his difficult slave Yaff for sale in 1835. Monmouth Democrat *via Newspapers.com.*

Nicholas Disbrow also owned a stagecoach business for transporting people arriving by ship from New York at the Keyport dock to locations in coastal Middlesex and Monmouth Counties. He died in 1864, before the Thirteenth Amendment abolished slavery, but Disbrow must have had difficulty reconciling himself with the slavery legislation, which caused such large societal changes. His Middletown Point Daybooks, which are preserved in the Monmouth County Historical Association archives, contain details of his transactions with his many customers and tradespeople. He often described free Black adult workmen as "colored boys."

OUR NEW JERSEY STATE university, Rutgers in New Brunswick, is not exempt from involvement with slavery. The Reverend Theodorus Frelinghuysen, father of one of the university's founders, purchased a slave for fifty pounds in New York in the early eighteenth century, before bringing the man to Raritan. We know about this enslaved man because he published an autobiography. His life story has some interesting parallels to that of Lewis Morris's personal servant, Yaff.

The man enslaved to Reverend Frelinghuysen was named James A. Ukawsaw Gronniosaw. He was born in Africa around 1710, the grandson of a king. When Gronniosaw was fifteen, he was fooled into visiting the western Gold Coast, where he was enslaved. He was shipped to Barbados and sold

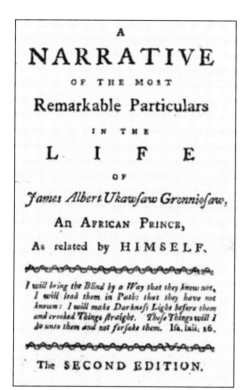

A

NARRATIVE

OF THE MOST

Remarkable Particulars

IN THE

L I F E

OF

James Albert Ukawsaw Gronniosaw,

An AFRICAN PRINCE,

As related by H I M S E L F.

I will bring the Blind by a Way that they know not, I will lead them in Paths that they have not known: I will make Darkness Light before them and crooked Things straight. These Things will I do unto them and not forsake them. Isa. xlii. 16.

The SECOND EDITION.

James A. Ukawsaw Gronniosaw wrote an autobiography about his amazing life of slavery and freedom on three continents during the eighteenth century. *A Narrative, Ukawsaw Gronniosaw, 1772.*

and then landed in New York City, where Frelinghuysen bought him. The Dutch Reformed churchman had the African tutored and converted to Christianity. Ukawsaw Gronniosaw remained conflicted between his origins and the new faith he was being pressured to adopt for the rest of his life.

As Gronniosaw related:

Mr. Freelandhouse [sic] took me home with him, and made me kneel down, and put my two hands together, and pray'd for me, and every night and morning he did the same. I could not make out what it was for, nor the meaning of it, nor what they spoke to when they talk'd. I thought it comical, but I lik'd it very well. After I had been a little while with my new master I grew more familiar, and ask'd him the meaning of prayer: (I could hardly speak English to be understood) he took great pains with me, and made me understand that he pray'd to God, who liv'd in Heaven; that He was my Father and BEST Friend. I told him that this must be a mistake; that my father liv'd at BOURNOU [present-day Nigeria], and I wanted very much to see him, and likewise my dear mother, and sister, and I wish'd he would be so good as to send me home to them.

Of course, that was the furthest thing, and the farthest place, on Frelinghuysen's mind for his slave.

The resilient Gronniosaw persevered and grew to like his master and family. Frelinghuysen died in 1747, freeing Gronniosaw on his deathbed. The former slave confessed that "the loss of Mr. Freelandhouse distress'd me greatly." He continued to serve the family as a domestic servant for years, no doubt the best choice he saw for himself. Gronniosaw was present when a son of the Reverend Frelinghuysen and others began discussions for their vision of a Dutch college in America. Queen's College was chartered in 1766 and renamed Rutgers College in 1825.

Gronniosaw's life took another turn when the last of his Frelinghuysen employers died. Threatened with imminent enslavement, he fled. Wandering through the Caribbean for a few years, he worked as a cook and a British soldier. He went to Spain, London and spent a year in Amsterdam as a butler. He eventually settled in England, where he married a poor white servant girl with whom he had three children. Ukawsaw Gronniosaw died in 1775.

For an enslaved and displaced African who endured so much, Gronniosaw paradoxically embraced the American and European mores thrust upon him. Though he always yearned for his lost African life, he saw his later years through Christian eyes when he wrote:

> *Though the Grandson of a King, I have wanted bread, and should have been glad of the hardest crust I ever saw. I who, at home, was surrounded and guarded by slaves, so that no indifferent person might approach me, and clothed with gold, have been inhumanly threatened with death…yet I never murmured, nor was I discontented. I am willing, and even desirous to be counted as nothing, a stranger in the world, and a pilgrim here; for "I know that my REDEEMER liveth" and I'm thankful for every trial and trouble that I've met with, as I am not without hope that they have been all sanctified to me.*

Part II.

WEST JERSEY

6

GEORGE WASHINGTON'S SLAVES; HUNTERDON AND MORRIS COUNTIES

You got to move, child,
You got to move.
But when the Lord gets ready
You got to move.
—Mississippi Fred McDowell, "You Got to Move"

W ithin a month of Lewis Morris's appointment as the first royal colonial
governor of New Jersey in 1738, Morris County was carved out of
Hunterdon County. It was a political tribute to Morris, who had played a
large role in the separation of New Jersey from New York, as they were
governed as one entity for many years.

During the Revolutionary War, General George Washington spent
considerable time in Hunterdon County and other parts of New Jersey.
Several of his slaves are noteworthy, not only for the time they were with him
in New Jersey but also for how differently they were treated. Washington was
not an insignificant slaveholder. At his Mount Vernon estate in Virginia, the
man who became our first president kept over 300 slaves—124 of his own
and the rest belonging to his wife, Martha.

Many of our founding fathers were slaveholders. Most egregious of all
was Thomas Jefferson ("all men are created equal"), who after the death
of his wife had a long-term relationship with her half-sister, his slave Sally
Hemings.

LE GÉNÉRAL WASHINGTON

Ne Quid Detrimenti capiat Res publica.

The slave William "Billy" Lee (*background with horse*) was George Washington's personal servant throughout the Revolutionary War and later at Mount Vernon in Virginia. *Library of Congress.*

George Washington purchased William "Billy" Lee, son of an enslaved mother and a white father, for sixty-one pounds in 1768. Lee was Washington's personal "servant" during and after the time he led the Continental army in the Revolutionary War. He performed a myriad of functions for Washington, acting as his valet, messenger and personal secretary.

Lee's many years of intimate service for Washington might have caused the president to soften some of his views on slavery, but not all. For instance, Washington initially resisted Lee's request to bring his wife to Mount Vernon after the war. This is especially odd since Margaret Thomas was a free Black woman who'd been a laundress and seamstress in the traveling wartime household. Though Washington eventually acquiesced to Billy Lee's request, there is no record of Margaret working at Mount Vernon. She might have died before she ever made it to Virginia.

Though Billy Lee remained enslaved during Washington's lifetime, the general public acknowledged his special status. He was so well known that visitors to Mount Vernon after the war often wanted to meet the "famed body-servant of the commander-in-chief."

———

ANOTHER WASHINGTON SLAVE SUFFERED an entirely different fate. In a book published 120 years after the fact, New Jersey writer Frank R. Stockton reported that when Washington was in Morristown in 1777, an unidentified aide wrote:

> *The General will esteem it as a singular favor if you can apprehend a mulatto girl, servant and slave of Mrs. Washington, who eloped from this place yesterday, with what design cannot be conjectured, though as she may intend to the enemy and pass your way I trouble you with the description: her name is Charlotte but in all probability will change it, yet may be discovered by question. She is light complected* [sic], *about thirteen years of age, pert, dressed in brown cloth wescoat* [sic] *and petticoat. Your falling upon some method of recovering her should she be near you will accommodate Mrs. Washington and lay her under great obligations to you being the only female servant she brought from home and intending to be off to-day had she not been missing. A gentle reward will be given to any soldier or other who shall take her up.*

> *I am with respect your most obedient servant.*

Unfortunately, Stockton did not identify his source for the letter, nor enough detail to determine if this runaway was the same Charlotte found on a roster of slaves at Mount Vernon years later. But during her time working at the Virginia estate, the seamstress Charlotte reported that she had been whipped around the time of the reported escape, so perhaps it was she who was recaptured and punished.

GEORGE WASHINGTON APPARENTLY WANTED to free his Mount Vernon slaves in his 1799 will. His intention was complicated because over half of them—dower slaves Martha Dandridge Custis brought into this second marriage—belonged to his wife. He could not control their fate:

> *Upon the decease of my wife, it is my Will & desire that all the Slaves which I hold in my own right, shall receive their freedom. To emancipate them during her life, would, tho' earnestly wished by me, be attended with such insuperable difficulties on account of their intermixture by Marriages*

George and Martha Washington owned three hundred slaves at their Mount Vernon estate. *Junius Brutus Stearns painting, 1851.*

with the dower Negroes, as to excite the most painful sensations, if not disagreeable consequences from the latter, while both descriptions are in the occupancy of the same Proprietor; it not being in my power, under the tenure by which the Dower Negroes are held, to manumit them. And whereas among those who will recieve [sic] freedom according to this devise, there may be some, who from old age or bodily infirmities, and others who on account of their infancy, that will be unable to support themselves.

Washington did recognize his special debt to Billy Lee, the only slave freed in his will:

And to my Mulatto man William (calling himself William Lee) I give immediate freedom; or if he should prefer it (on account of the accidents which have befallen him, and which have rendered him incapable of walking or of any active employment) to remain in the situation he now is, it shall be optional in him to do so: In either case however, I allow him an annuity of thirty dollars during his natural life, which shall be independent of the victuals and cloaths [sic] he has been accustomed to receive, if he chuses [sic] the last alternative; but in full, with his freedom, if he prefers the first; & this I give him as a testimony of my sense of his attachment to me, and for his faithful services during the Revolutionary War.

In December 1800, Martha Washington signed a deed of manumission for her deceased husband's slaves. Her dower slaves would have to wait for their freedom.

———•———

MARTHA CUSTIS WASHINGTON'S OWN attitude toward her slaves was evident in this statement she made in 1795: "The Blacks are so bad in their nature that they have not the least gratitude for the kindness that may be shewed to them." Nothing exemplifies Martha's abhorrent feelings toward her slaves much more than her long-term quest to find another of her escaped women, Ona Maria Judge.

Oney Judge ran away from Martha while the Washingtons were living in Philadelphia in May 1796. ("Oney" was the kind of diminutive slaveholders used to infantilize their slaves, similar to how they called grown Black men "boy.") The twenty-three-year-old Judge, Martha's personal maid and seamstress, expected to be freed when her mistress died. Judge walked away after hearing that she'd remain enslaved even after Martha's death.

Claypoole's American Daily Advertiser noted the ten-dollar reward and described Judge as having "absconded from the household of the President of the United States....A light mulatto girl, much freckled, with very black eyes and bushy black hair, she is of middle stature, and delicately formed."

With the ignorance of runaway motivations so common among slaveholders, the ad continued, "As there was no suspicion of her going off, nor no provocation to do so, it is not easy to conjecture whither she has gone, or fully, what her design is."

George Washington had signed the Fugitive Slave Act in 1793—"An Act respecting fugitives from justice, and persons escaping from the service of their masters." The federal law allowed slave owners, or their surrogate bounty hunters, to pursue, capture and return runaway

Ona "Oney" Judge was Martha Washington's twenty-three-year-old slave who ran away to New Hampshire in 1796. *Fred W. Smith National Library for the Study of George Washington.*

slaves even in "free" states. Anyone helping these escaped slaves was subject to criminal penalties and a $500 fine.

Ona Judge's escape might have been aided by the free Black abolitionist community in the City of Brotherly Love, a precursor to William Still's Underground Railroad activities in the nineteenth century (which we examine in chapter 9). Judge probably took a ship from the Philadelphia docks down the Delaware River and then up the Jersey coast to her eventual destination of Portsmouth, New Hampshire. Ona Judge eluded the Washingtons' vindictive efforts to get her back for years.

When the Washingtons finally located her, Ona Judge said she'd return if she was manumitted when Martha died. George Washington replied that her demand was "totally inadmissible" on the grounds that such a deal would "reward unfaithfulness," and besides, it would encourage others "far more deserving of favor." Ona went into hiding again.

Judge refused to leave New Hampshire and created as normal a life as possible under her circumstances. She married John Staines, and they lived

George and Martha Washington at Mount Vernon with their adoptive children, George Washington Parke Custis and Nelly Custis, and their slave William Lee. *Edward Savage painting, 1789, National Gallery of Art.*

close to poverty with three children. But Ona did succeed in living out her life as a "free" woman, though she was technically never emancipated. Ona Judge Staines died in Greenland, New Hampshire, in 1848.

In a sad denouement to their often-unfeeling relationships with their enslaved women and men, neither George nor Martha Washington ever fully embraced the principles of equality for all people. George was deeply involved in determining the status of slaves who had run away to the British side during the war. He was insistent that these slaves were "property" and needed to be returned to their owners. Martha Washington, who died three years after her husband, included this bequest in her will: "I give to my grandson George Washington Parke Custis my mulato [*sic*] man Elish—that I bought of Mr. Butler Washington to him and his heir forever." Thus the former first lady of the United States ensured the man's continuing enslavement.

Grandson "Wash" Parke Custis was twenty-one years old when Martha Washington died. He attended the College of New Jersey (now Princeton

University) for a time but didn't graduate. His attitude toward slaves was the same as his family's—they were to be used at his pleasure. He fathered two daughters by two different slave women who had once been owned by the Washingtons.

———·———

THE ABOMINATION THAT WAS slavery permeated all levels of New Jersey society in the eighteenth century. It was especially prevalent among the rich, many of whom would not have achieved their wealth without slave labor. The Pitney family, who lived and prospered in Mendham Township beginning in the 1720s, are one such example. For the ensuing two centuries, Pitneys became wealthy businessmen, jurists and politicians. Henry Cooper Pitney published the first comprehensive history of Morris County in 1914.

Henry Pitney's great-grandfather James Pitney was involved in a notable legal matter settled by New Jersey's highest court in 1793. Three years before "the State against James Pitney of the County of Morris" made it to the state supreme court, James Pitney purchased a thirteen-year-old Black boy, also named James. The enslaved James was the son of a woman named Juddy. Young as the boy was, James Pitney thought he would be a valuable farmhand on the large Pitney property. But the sale was complicated because the boy's mother had been manumitted in the final will of her owner, Jasper Smith.

Though Juddy was freed years before Pitney bought her son, Smith's heirs contended that the young James was a slave when he was sold. In its decision, which predated New Jersey's Act for the Gradual Abolition of Slavery by a decade, the supreme court noted:

> *No Bond or other Security whatsoever was given by the said Jasper Smith, the Master of the said young Juddy and testator in the Will above named, pursuant to the Act of Assembly passed 16ᵗʰ November 1769...[and] having taken due consideration, are unanimously of Opinion, that the said Negro Juddy was "a free woman by the Will of the said Jasper Smith."... Consequently the said James her Son is entitled to his Freedom, and do therefore order, that the said James be discharged from the illegal Detention of the said James Pitney, and he is discharged accordingly.*

James Pitney's son Mahlon was also involved in an infamous legal case. Mahlon was a militiaman who served under George Washington during the Revolutionary War. His case concerned the brutal treatment of a slave owned by a man named Abraham Cooper of Chester, a town ten miles west of Mendham.

Though slaves in New Jersey were always subject to harsh and frequently legal treatment, Cooper had gone too far in 1808. He beat his slave Cato for some minor issue and then branded the man's forehead. Mahlon Pitney was foreman of the jury that tried Cooper. The jurors found that Cato had been "grievously wounded and hurt" and experienced "great pain, torture, and other wrong." Nonetheless, Cooper was fined a mere forty dollars. Though not an insignificant amount of money at the time, Cooper's punishment was a trifle compared to the scarred appearance Cato had to endure for the rest of his life.

Based on the judgement rendered in the Cato case alone, we might be inclined to think Mahlon Pitney was sympathetic to the plight of enslaved people. Yet, Morris County records show that Mahlon Pitney registered the birth of a baby called Peg, born to "my negro slave named Rachel" just two years later. Clearly, severe injury inflicted on a slave was one thing, but owning slaves was another and a very acceptable notion to men of that era.

———◦———

THE *NEW JERSEY FREEMAN* was an antislavery newspaper published in Boonton between 1844 and 1850. Despite its high-minded abolitionist views, one particular article reflects prevalent contemporary biases. An anonymous writer calling himself the "Advocate of Moral Reform" thought slaves, though worthy of freedom, were still not quite equal to white people.

The December 1844 story in the paper concerned the poignant love between two slaves, William and Lucy. The pair were separated when the woman was purchased by a married white man to be his "intended paramour." The "advocate" wrote:

> *William was a slave…*a mullato *of fine appearance and* uncommon intelligence, *and as the coachman of his master enjoyed many privileges denied to others* of his class; *he had informed an attachment for* a young Quadroon, *who was the personal attendant of her mistress, and who had profited to the utmost by the few opportunities afforded her, so that in mind and manners she was far superior to many who looked down upon her as slave, with contempt. Her personal appearance was likewise,*

uncommonly attractive, *and* poor William *soon found that though his attachment was warmly returned, and she had become his wife according to* the simple form recognized among slaves, *his claims to the chosen of his heart were not likely to be undisputed.* [emphasis is author's]

William liberated Lucy from an Alabama plantation, and the couple spent months following "the star of freedom [which] pointed to the north." Alas, Lucy died along the way, and William continued alone to Philadelphia and then through the mid–New Jersey section of the Underground Railroad on his way to New York. He eventually reached "the British dominions" of Canada, where he was "established in a good business."

Despite its unintentional slights, this tale, written in the florid journalistic style of the pre–Civil War abolitionist press, is full of pathos, concluding with an appeal to see slaves as human beings: "But it is manifest to the casual observer that he has been a man of sorrow, and those who have heard his sad story, well known, that whatever objects may claim a passing interest, his heart is buried with Lucy, in that grave in the wilderness, where she sleeps in the dark and distant forest of eastern Maryland."

7

DUTCH AND ENGLISH EXPANSION OF SLAVERY INTO SOMERSET COUNTY

Hey listen mama,
The world is done gone away.
I've got a bad luck deal,
Give me trouble every day.
—*Frank Stokes, "Downtown Blues"*

S omerset County, officially chartered in May 1688, is in the middle of northern New Jersey, bounded by Hunterdon and Mercer Counties to its west and Union and Middlesex to the east. Like many New Jersey locales, Somerset County shares its name with its English antecedent. And likewise, from its earliest days, Somerset embraced the attitudes of its founding settlers toward slavery.

The first Europeans arrived in Somerset around 1681 and began farming around present-day Bound Brook. These English/Scots and Dutch settlers depended on slaves for labor-intensive farm work. As more land came under development, the slave population increased, as did the problems caused by subjugating people.

During the eighteenth century, a series of incidents alarmed Somerset County slaveholders, always worried as much about their physical safety as their financial well-being. Reacting to typically harsh treatment and rumors that they might be freed, Somerville slaves were suspected of plotting an uprising in 1734. For white slave masters, this was all too reminiscent of the very real 1712 New York City slave revolt. The Somerville slaves' alleged plan was for hundreds of bondmen to burn their masters' houses and barns, murder their oppressors and steal horses during one coordinated night of terror. In the aftermath, the conspirators hoped to flee to safety by joining up with Native Americans.

Though the threat was scary enough, the slaveholders were further enraged by the impudence of an intoxicated slave who challenged a white man, saying that "he was as good a Man." This assumption by a Black man that he had equal human status was considered a grievous affront. Colonial white people "knew" their slaves were nothing but "barbarous monsters." The slave's intemperate remark, and his follow-up assertion that the white man would soon find out what he meant, led to the plot's exposure. Swift retribution followed—hangings, disfigurements and whippings of the leaders. Extreme violence was always the go-to reaction of slaveholders.

MICHAEL VAN VEGHTEN WAS an early Dutch settler who bought hundreds of acres of "Raritan River Lotts" from the East Jersey Proprietors near today's Bridgewater. He donated some of his land for the Reformed Dutch Church of Raritan. Whatever the depth of his religious feelings, it did not preclude him from being the first of several generations of his family who would hold people in bondage against their will. Van Veghten's namesake grandson filed several documents as part of legally required responses to New Jersey's Act for the Gradual Abolition of Slavery of 1804.

In 1817, grandson Michael Van Veghten noted there "was born in my family a female black Child...by the Name of Sarah Elizabeth." Sarah was considered a family member, albeit clearly inferior, while she lived at the Van Veghten homestead.

Four years later, Van Veghten registered another birth stating, "Sir, Be pleased to enter on your records of the birth of colored children the Name of Harry Thomas who was born in my family on Sunday June 16th, 1822." This filing occurred three months after the law required, but the audacious Van Veghten deflected blame for his being tardy with this note: "This has been so long omitted that I must inform you that by forgetfulness & the indecision of the parents about the child's name has been the cause of it."

Van Veghten also registered the births of three other unnamed slaves who he inherited from his father, Derrick. We don't know how many slaves

Top: Slaveholder Michael Van Veghten built his home near Bridgewater in Somerset County. *Library of Congress.*

Bottom: This Van Veghten slave birth recording was required by New Jersey's 1804 Act for the Gradual Abolition of Slavery. *Somerset County Clerk's Office.*

were ultimately bought or sold by the Van Veghten family. Even allowing for inevitable deaths or sales of some of them, we have only an approximation of the number of Van Veghten–owned slaves over three generations. As property, slaves were afterthoughts.

GUISBERT BOGART, A DUTCHMAN who lived along the Raritan River in Somerset County in the late eighteenth century, owned a man named Samuel Sutphin, who was born around 1747. After Bogart died, Samuel had a succession of masters: Casper Berger (Readington, Hunterdon County), Peter Ten Eyck (North Branch), the Reverend John Duryea (pastor of the Dutch Reformed Church, Somerville) and finally Peter Sutphin (Bedminster).

The slave Samuel Sutphin served as a Revolutionary War soldier in place of Casper Berger, who'd purchased him for about ninety-two pounds from Bogart. In exchange for substituting for Berger, Samuel was promised his freedom. Sutphin's remembrances as an eighty-five-year-old man living in Bernards Township were preserved in an 1830s manuscript. It was recorded for the illiterate slave by Dr. Lewis Condict. Condict personally interviewed many Revolutionary War veterans to help them get their deserved war pensions.

Samuel Sutphin served a number of tours in the Continental militia. He recalled that the first was after "Berger bought me in the season plane [*sic*] seed sowing....Immediately after I had finished planting 4 acres corn....I took my turn with others." Samuel and other soldiers were marched through Bound Brook, Scotch Plains, Newark and finally Communipaw in Bergen County (Jersey City). During his monthlong stay at Communipaw, Samuel was engaged in building breastworks, observation positions across the river from New York.

Sutphin related that on a second tour, he took part in the Battle of Long Island (August 1776) when the British routed Washington's army in Brooklyn. Sutphin escaped on a small boat to Staten Island and took three days to return to his home. In subsequent actions, Samuel Sutphin was stationed at Communipaw again, Readington, Princeton and Rocky Hill. He also recalled that George Washington took winter quarters near Pluckemin. Samuel Sutphin was one of at least twenty Black men appearing on a list of New Jersey soldiers at the Battle of Monmouth in June 1782, although Condict doesn't mention Sutphin's participation in that pivotal battle. As many as 750 Black soldiers fought in the Continental army on that hot summer day.

Periodically during spring seasons, Sutphin would resume his planting duties before marching off again for other campaigns. Sutphin was engaged in operations in upstate New York and claimed he killed a Hessian soldier while he was on guard duty at West Point on the Hudson. He was wounded twice during that action, "both wounds or scars yet visible and tangible" years later. Condict reported that Sutphin said Berger sold him for £192 to Ten Eyck, who sold him to Duryea for £92 and then for the same amount to Peter Sutphin. Samuel bought his freedom from Peter Sutphin for £92.

Samuel Sutphin apparently spoke Dutch, reflecting his original owner's heritage, and thus needed help with his pension applications. Perhaps he spoke broken English, too, which may account for misspellings and variations of people and places he remembered. He was illiterate. The errors might be those of a clerk taking notes during Samuel's testimony or possibly mistakes made by Dr. Condict, writing what he thought he heard. The slave's own name was sometimes spelled as Sutphen.

Dr. Condict, trying to influence the War Department favorably on Samuel's behalf, said the former slave "is now and has been for years, a communicant, in good standing in the Baskingridge [sic] Church, a sober, industrious, meek, humble and devout Christian whose unassuming walk and consistent deportment would put to the blush, many a lofty look."

Because he had little documentation of his military service, and due to the inconsistencies in his testimony, Samuel Sutphin's application for pension was denied repeatedly. White veteran applicants with less detailed service records did receive relief, so it's hard to escape the conclusion that Sutphin was denied his compensation simply because he was a Black man. A very old former slave with mixed memories didn't get any benefit of doubt.

To add further insult, Sutphin didn't receive the freedom he'd been promised. Similar to the experiences of the many New Jersey runaway slaves who served with the British army during the Revolutionary War, the Patriot soldier and wounded veteran Samuel Sutphin's military sacrifices were just that—sacrifices with no reward. Ultimately, Samuel Sutphin realized he'd have to purchase his own dignity. He testified that "from the proceeds of my labor...I paid it and bought my freedom after the additional servitude of 20 years under different masters."

———•———

AROUND 1786, AARON MALICK of Bedminster bought a slave named Yombo from his brother-in-law. Malick wanted Yombo's skills as a leather tanner for his business. The details of Yombo's life appear in a manuscript called "The Story of an Old Farm," written by Malick's great-grandson Andrew

Mellick in 1889. Malick's descendant offered his version of the relationship between the enslaved man and his owner as a kind of apologia, putting the best possible spin on an obviously untoward reality.

Mellick began his family tale by pointing out that Aaron Malick "was an old man before he became a slaveholder…at a time when Aaron was sorely pressed for help." Apparently, Malick had overcome the strong objections to Yombo's purchase by his wife, Charlotte, whose Quaker family opposed slavery.

Yombo said he was captured as a young boy in Guinea, but Malick dismissed the man's claim that his father was a "big man," an important African king. The slave was described as "stout, coal black, club-footed and very bow-legged. At first his appearance quite terrified…children." Yombo is described as illiterate and an incorrigible thief. Malick often caught Yombo stealing his leather goods to sell for the support of the slave's wife, who lived separately from him in Elizabethtown. Besides chewing tobacco and wearing rings in his ears, Yombo's "disposition was not in any sense agreeable, and his perverseness always displayed itself when he was not under the immediate eye of his owner and master." Yombo's supposed deficits—"notwithstanding his master's goodness the darkey was treacherous"—were taken in stride because he was such a valuable worker.

From the physical description and behaviors of Yombo, readers were meant to understand that this slave was deformed and different-looking, something less than a normal human being (he had probably been hobbled by the chains and restraints during his capture); that he had weird adornments (African rings in his ears); that he did not speak proper English (quite true, he was from Guinea); that he was defiant (a natural reaction to his enslavement); and that he never recognized the "kindnesses" bestowed on him by his understanding master (such as what? Allowing Yombo to take a carriage to see his wife?).

Despite the demeaning conditions of their lives and the punishments Yombo and other Malick slaves were forced to endure, "The Story of an Old Farm" purports that "slavery on the 'Old Farm' was not altogether cruel, or unusual: For a number of years much happiness in their mutual relations came to both bond and free; their lives moved on with but little friction, excepting an occasional outbreak from Yombo, which was met by a few earnest words of reproof from Aaron, who even in extreme old age retained the spirit of mastery."

When Aaron Malick died in 1809, Mellick wrote, the disposition of slaves in his will was the result of "much anxious thought on his part." Obviously cognizant of the 1804 Gradual Abolition Law, Malick stated in his will the wish that his slaves be sold "under indenture" until they reached the appropriate ages. This was "evidently a compromise of the old gentleman's between his children and his slaves." Why would this slaveholder be so accommodating? Mellick said, "Had he freed his negroes it would have meant pauperism for them, and an incubus for his estate, as they would have had to be supported."

On May 23, 1809, an auction was held where seven slaves, boys, girls, women and men, were sold for from $35 to $225. "Then came under the hammer poor old Yombo, bending under the weight of his seventy years… sold a slave to John Hastier for $50. The sale over, Yombo goes contentedly to his new home." Several years later, Yombo died in Elizabethtown.

Mellick's book was a deliberate attempt, just a few decades after slavery was abolished in the United States, to reimagine the dreadful institution of chattel bondage as a myth of paternalism. Mellick's was only one of the many post–Thirteenth Amendment justifications written about slavery, seeking to repaint it—to literally whitewash it—as a necessary but benign evil. This was a kind of *Gone with the Wind* for New Jersey. Despite Andrew Mellick's attempt to paint his ancestor as a benevolent slaveholder, no Malicks appear in the nineteenth-century slave births or manumission records of Somerset County.

These and other revisionist portrayals of slavery in New Jersey were told strictly from the white slaveholder's vantage point for white readers. While it might be understandable, though hardly excusable, that a descendant of a slaveholder would write a positive biography, these narratives took hold in the popular imagination as truth. Winners write history, and the histories written by and for northern state consumption made the rebellious Confederacy the locus of evil slavery. During the twentieth century, New Jersey schoolchildren were rarely exposed to the awful reality that had transpired in the Garden State. The fable of northern righteousness took hold.

Newer scholarship, by both Black and white researchers and historians, provides a more nuanced and realistic view of how slavery felt to the enslaved. For example, scholar Kenneth E. Marshall's 2011 analysis of the Yombo-Malick relationship cuts through the haze of guilty fantasy to the abject abomination that was slavery. Marshall's *Manhood Enslaved: Bondmen in Eighteenth- and Early Nineteenth-Century New Jersey* elucidates how New Jersey slavery was every bit as harsh and horrible as elsewhere in the United States.

And then we have this contradictory story of Aaron Malick to consider. In 1801, he sold a small plot of land to three Black man. The trio—a freeman

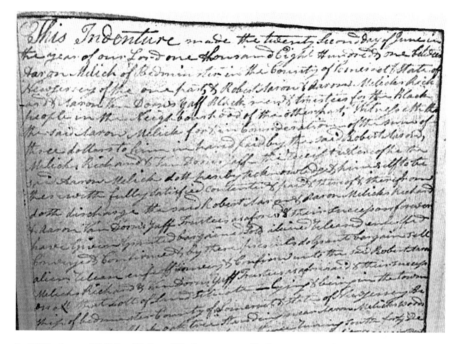

In 1801, Aaron Malick sold three Black men a small plot to use as a burial ground. *"The Story of an Old Farm,"* 1889.

named Robert Aaron and the slaves Richard and Yaff—paid three dollars for it. The deed of sale indicates that the men were "trustees for the Black people in the Neighborhood of Bedminster and their Successors forever for the use and purpose of a burying ground for the said Black people in the said neighborhood."

Andrew Mellick recalled passing the site a half century later. During a horse-and-carriage ride on a country road to visit the Old Farm, Mellick wrote, "Before reaching it we pass a neglected 'God's-Acre.' It is the simple burial place of slaves and their posterity who once formed an important element of the work-a-day world of this township. The headstones, if there ever were any, have long since disappeared; the decrepit fences are covered with a rambling growth of weeds and creeping vines."

Over time, in an all-too-typical story of the neglect of important African American historical sites in New Jersey, the tiny property passed to Bedminster Township. The town hall was built over the resting place of these souls. By the twenty-first century, after the municipal building was torn down, officials considered selling the twenty-two-square-yard cemetery—one of the first freemen's burial grounds in the United States.

Unable to find a buyer, and with a lack of interest of the town's citizens for turning it into a small park, the cemetery site was plowed under and seeded with grass. Like the people buried there, the importance of the place might have been lost forever.

Fortunately, Thomas L. Buckingham of the Somerset County Historical Society researched the property deeds, comparing them with the burial records of Bedminster's Dutch Reform Church. Buckingham estimated that about fifty people were interred in the small 0.1-acre plot. He identified these eight former slaves by name:

Betty Bullion, died on May 24, 1841
Ellen Wortman, twelve, died on August 17, 1842
Margaret Sloan, twenty-seven, died on June 17, 1842
Harry (no last name), died on September 20, 1849
Sarah Cox, infant, died on January 22, 1844
Jack Suydam, seventy-nine, died on January 8, 1850
Margaret Sutphen, eight, died on March 27, 1845
Loney Sloan, seventy-six, died on April 19, 1848

Due to the efforts of the Somerset County Historical Society and the Bedminster Historical Preservation Commission, a historical marker was erected on the Hillside Avenue burying ground in 2014, two hundred years

The long-neglected, two-hundred-year-old historic African American cemetery in Bedminster was finally recognized with this plaque erected in 2014. *Rick Geffken.*

after its first burial. Andrew Mellick had written about the small graveyard: "The rains of many years have beaten level the humble mounds of the dusky toilers." When this author visited the site on a rainy wintry day in 2020, it was once again a lonely thicket of weeds, strikingly barren in a neighborhood that now features many well-kept homes.

THE 1804 GRADUAL ABOLITION Act required slaveholders to file two types of documents at their county courthouse. The first was a "Birth Record," a kind of placeholder to establish when these newborns would be eligible for manumission—twenty-one years later for women, twenty-five years for men. Perhaps half of these "slaves for a term" lived long enough to see their freedom. A second filing was supposed to be made when the slave was actually granted freedom. More often than not, the manumission document gave the freed person's name.

Two overseers of the poor and two justices of the peace were required to sign certificates attached to the manumission documents. These functionaries would verify that the slave owner presented the slave "who, on view and examination, appears to be sound in mind, and not under any bodily incapacity of obtaining a support, and also is not under the age of twenty-one years nor above the age of forty years." The authorities wanted to make sure manumitted slaves were self-supporting and would place no financial burdens on local government. This was the latest version of requirements that first appeared in a 1714 law mandating slave owners to pay £200 for each manumitted slave. It was modified in 1786, so former owners were no longer obligated to pay for a freed person's upkeep. The 1804 act saw to it that newly freed slaves received no monetary compensations or reparations—their freedom was thought to be gift enough.

Examinations of the Black birth records in Somerset County show Dutch settlers were the largest group of slaveholders between 1805 and 1840. Among these were Martin Voorhees (who registered the birth of Patty to Betty and Cesar in April 1806); Hendrick Suydam (registered Aaron, son of Peg in January 1805); and Douwe Ditmas (registered Jude, born to Bette in June 1805).

Although most of the birth recordings use identical pro forma language copied from a clerk's sample, there are other revealing phrasings. In October 1805, Bernadine Van Zandt records, "Phebe born of a Wench

COUNTY BUILDINGS SOMERVILLE.

In 1804, New Jersey required slaveholders to register slave births and manumissions at county courthouses like this one in Somerset. *Somerset County map, 1850.*

called Sara being my property." Van Zandt and most other slaveholders saw their slaves as machines whose only purpose was to make their owners' lives easier and profitable.

After 1823, the Somerset manumission records indicate the changing nationality makeup of the county—many more English slaveholders appear, with names such as Baker, Higgins, Miller, Smith, Thompson and the like. Dutch slaveholders are still represented. Michael Van Veghten, for one, freed Jack in 1825 and then James in 1831.

THE SOURLAND MOUNTAIN AREA of West Jersey stretches across Somerset and Mercer Counties. The small communities of Zion and Skillman are in southwest Somerset. Free and formerly enslaved Black people established the Mount Zion AME (African Methodist Episcopal) Church just after passage of the Thirteenth Amendment. Just a few years ago, Beverly Mills and Elaine Buck started to research the history of the church and the cemetery. The two women recently published *If These Stones Could Talk* about the African American influence in the area and founded the Stoutsburg Sourland African American Museum, housed in the old AME church.

Many of the church's parishioners and their ancestors are buried at the associated Stoutsburg Cemetery in Hopewell Township. For many years, New Jersey state law prohibited burying Black people at the same cemeteries with whites, continuing legal segregation even after death. The Negro Burial Bill of 1884 changed that absurd legislation. Our first president, George Washington, has a supporting role in the story of this burial ground.

The iconic Leutze painting of *Washington Crossing the Delaware* in 1776 depicts a Black man, possibly William Stives, just in front of George Washington. Washington Crossing the Delaware, *by Emanuel Leutze, 1851.*

During the Revolutionary War, a free Black man named William Stives (1760–1839) enlisted as a fifer in the Third New Jersey Regiment. He might have been enslaved at one time. Stives crossed the Delaware River with George Washington on Christmas night 1776. (In his iconic and apocryphal 1851 painting, artist Emanuel Leutze might have meant the Black man portrayed manning the oars directly in front of Washington to represent the several known to participate during that cold December evening: William Stives; the general's slave Billy Lee; or possibly Prince Whipple, a slave to one of Washington's aides.)

William Stives also spent that terrible winter of 1777–78 with General Washington at Valley Forge. After the war, Stives settled in the Hopewell area and married Catherine Vanois in 1789. The couple remained together for fifty years while they raised their family in this mountainous region of New Jersey. As a Baptist, William Stives was probably not buried at the Stoutsburg Cemetery, but one of his descendants nonetheless placed a commemorative marker to him there.

Also laid to rest at the Stoutsburg Cemetery are ten Civil War veterans documented as U.S. Colored Troops. Remarkably, these Black men and others had to enlist elsewhere because New Jersey refused to organize its own Black troops. They trained at Camp William Penn, a historical irony, since Penn himself was a slaveholder.

The ten men from the Sourland Mountain area who served honorably were Raymond Bergen, William Boyer, George Dillon, Lewis Fisher, William Reasoner, Samuel Ridley, James Schenk, Jonathan Stives, Aaron Truehart and John VanZandt.

Author Beverly Mills grew up in Hopewell. She brings her unique insight and perspective about the historical reality of New Jersey slavery in her book with Elaine Buck. They found a 1765 newspaper ad wherein a Cornelius Polhamus of Hopewell offered to sell "a Negroe Wench, this Country born, about 15 years of Age, and understands all kinds of Housework." Mills wrote:

> *I think about these people and what fate had in store for them. I recall myself as a fifteen-year-old Black female and put myself in the position of this girl-child who was being sold "for want of employ." She understood all kinds of housework and was clearly a marketable piece of property. I think about the man who literally held her life in his hands. Whom would she end up with and what treatment would she be subjected to by her new employer? The truth, as difficult as it is to face, is that New Jersey upheld the cruel system of slavery and was [as] entrenched in it as any southern state.*

8

MERCER COUNTY

SLAVERY IN NEW JERSEY'S CAPITAL

How many more years, are you gonna wreck my life?
Well the way you done, you gonna wreck my life.
—*Chester Arthur Burnett, also known as Howlin' Wolf, "No Place to Go"*

Mercer County was formed in 1838 from portions of Burlington, Hunterdon, Middlesex and Somerset. Trenton and Princeton, a mere dozen miles from each other, are the two most important towns in Mercer County. The former has been the state capital since 1790; the latter is the location of New Jersey's only Ivy League university (founded as the College of New Jersey in 1746). From their beginnings, both Trenton and Princeton attracted the well-to-do and the politically connected; thus, each owns a legacy of slavery.

Mahlon Stacy Sr., a Quaker, was the first to settle in what became Nottingham Township. He owned at least "four Negros" when he died in April 1704. His widow, Rebecca, manumitted her "negar woman Jane" seven years later. In her will, Rebecca Stacy also bequeathed Jane £20 yearly for life. Mrs. Stacy's inventory listed "three great bibles" and "two negro boys £100," whom she presumably did not free. Her son, Mahlon Stacy Jr., probably inherited the two young slaves.

Stacy Jr. sold eight hundred acres of his family's property at "Ye ffalles of ye De La Warr" to William Trent in 1714. The area was considered so unpromising that it was called Little Worth. Trent changed that when he took over Stacy's mill and, with the considerable labors of his own enslaved

TRENTON SUR LA DELAWARE

When William Trent moved to West Jersey, he chose a remote area near the falls of the Delaware River. It became the state capital, Trenton. *New York Historical Society.*

people, increased the agricultural productivity of the place. His Trent's-town eventually became Trenton. Our state capital's origin story is inseparable from slavery.

William Trent was already a rich Philadelphia merchant when he moved to the eastern side of the Delaware River to build his country estate in 1719. He brought his slaves with him. He had been politically active in Pennsylvania, part of its Provincial Council and one of the colony's supreme court judges. Trent was well connected with other prominent men, including the most important one, William Penn. Before he moved to West Jersey, Trent bought Penn's Schuylkill estate and rented a Philadelphia home called the Slate Roof House to the Pennsylvania colony's founder.

The source of Trent's wealth was his trading interests with Caribbean planters. Trent was a Quaker who bought and traded West Indian and African slaves. His preserved ledger gives a brief "account of Negroes." One entry from 1703 notes a purchase of four slaves for £130 from another Quaker, Samuel Carpenter.

OLD STACY MILL, ENLARGED AND IMPROVED BY WILLIAM TRENT,
AS IT APPEARED IN 1848, DILAPIDATED BY FIRE AND FLOOD.

Slaves worked this mill on the Assunpink Creek, first owned by Mahlon Stacy. William Trent
enlarged it and several others that produced flour, lumber and cloth. *Trenton Historical Society.*

Trent's road to riches was not unusual for Quaker merchants of his time.
In 1698, a colonial promoter wrote about numerous trade prospects with the
West Indies. "Negroes" were listed among other ordinary items in this list
of day-to-day commodities: "Their Merchandise chiefly consists in Horses,
Pipe-staves, Pork and Beef Salted and Barrelled up, Bread, and Flower, all
sorts of Grain, Pease, Beans, Skins, Furs, Tobacco, or Pot-Ashes, Wax, etc.,
which are Barter'd for Rumm, Sugar, Molasses, Silver, Negroes, Salt, Wine,
Linen, Household Goods, etc."

When William Trent died on Christmas Day in 1724, "being seized with a
fit of apoplexy," he owned these eleven slaves: "A man nam'd Yaff; a woman
nam'd Joan; a boy nam'd Bob; 1 D[itt]o Dick; a Girle Nanny; a child Tom.
Three Negro Men as follows Vizt. Julius, Bossin, Harry; Two Indian Men
Vizt. Cupid, Pedro." Though at first glance Trent might appear to be an
equal opportunity slave master, the "Two Indian Men" might actually have
been West Indian slaves.

Curiously, a century later, a book chronicling Philadelphia's history
contained this entry for 1738: "Three negro men were hung for poisoning
sundry persons in Jersey. They said they had poisoned Judge William Trent,
the founder of Trenton, among that number—but when he died none were
then suspected."

The three slaves supposedly hanged for the death of William Trent might have been victims of the resulting fear and frenzy generated by rumors of a 1736 slave rebellion in Antigua, West Indies. American colonists were constantly worried about their own slaves rising up.

———•———

IN 1738, LEWIS MORRIS was appointed the first royal colonial governor of New Jersey by King George II. When Morris and his wife, Isabella, moved to Trent's-town a few years later, they rented William Trent's old house from its then owner, the governor of Pennsylvania. The couple called their governor's mansion "Kingsbury Court."

Morris was the namesake nephew of a relocated Barbadian planter (discussed in chapter 2). Before he became a politician, he'd inherited the huge Tinton Manor estate from his uncle. Always ambitious, Morris vastly expanded his East Jersey holdings on his way to becoming one of the richest men in the Jerseys. The dozens of slaves he owned contributed immensely to the Morris family fortune.

Lewis Morris might have thought of his slaves as men and women, but he clearly placed them a step below white people. In a 1730 letter to his son John, then managing Tinton Manor, Lewis cautioned him "not to Trust negroes" because "they are both stupid and conceited and will follow their

TO GOVERNOR THOMAS.

Trenton Aprill 10ᵗʰ 1742

SIR:—If I remember your proposalls at Yates, concerning the letting of your house nigh this place, they were that you would expend £200 in putting of it into repaire & building of a wing for a kitchen to lodge servants : & would, so repair'd, let it with the grounds about it within fence for £60 per annum—that the lessee might cut his firewood, but not of timber trees—that there should be a lease for 5 yeares, & that if I became your tennant, the lease should determine within the 5 yeares, if either I dyed or his majestie was pleas'd to remove me from the government. I should have added another condition, w'ch tho' it may seem unlikely to many that it should happen, yet your experience has shewn it to be possible, & I believe it not improbable in case those I have to do with take it in their heads, w'ch I have abundant reason to think them capable of doing, & that is—withdrawing the house rent or sallary, w'ch if they do I shall be under a necessity of going to my own house, in w'ch case it would be hard to pay £60 per annum. [The repairs necessary are then referred to at some length.]

Before he moved to Trenton as governor, Lewis Morris wanted a kitchen built at the Trent House for his slaves. *Papers of Lewis Morris, 1852.*

Recent archaeological digs at the Trent House might locate Lewis Morris's slave quarters and kitchen. *Rick Geffken.*

own way if not carefully looked to." Generations of Morrises held fast to that biased belief.

Isabella Graham Morris was the daughter of a New York attorney. She was used to the privileges of the wealthy elite. After four decades spent as the wife of one of the most prominent men in New Jersey, the new first lady of New Jersey had no intentions of performing domestic tasks in a cold brick house on the banks of the Delaware. The Morrises brought some of their Tinton Manor slaves with them to Trenton.

Isabella Morris demanded that her husband put an outbuilding on the property for use as a kitchen and slave quarters. Lewis acquiesced to her in a 1742 letter he wrote to his landlord, George Thomas, asking for the outbuilding. Although we don't know how many slaves accompanied the Morrises to Trenton, nor their names, recent archaeological digs conducted by Hunter Research (Trenton) and Monmouth University (West Long Branch) might eventually locate the remains of the long-demolished kitchen and perhaps some clues to the slaves who lived there while they worked for the Morrises.

WILLIAM PENN GRANTED 5,500 acres of West Jersey land to Richard Stockton in 1701. His son John Stockton, who inherited the property, was also a founder of the College of New Jersey, which became Princeton University in 1896. John's son, Richard Stockton Jr., graduated as part of the college's first class. The younger Richard Stockton built a Princeton mansion house he called Morven during the late 1750s. Two centuries later, Morven became the first official residence of the governor of New Jersey. Stockton Jr. was a signer of the Declaration of Independence but built his fortune on the literal blood, sweat and tears of his many slaves.

Barring the discovery of a complete list of Stockton slaves, we can estimate that a dozen or so bondsmen and women were needed to maintain the three-hundred-plus-acre Stockton farm. Richard Stockton died while he was a captive of the British during the Revolutionary War in 1781. His will made no provision to free his enslaved men and women, but it did allow that his wife, Annis, "may free what slaves she wishes." She waited a few years before she saw fit to do so.

Annis Boudinot Stockton had an intriguing relationship with her slaves. She claimed to have wet-nursed a slave child named Marcus Marsh after the boy's mother died in 1765. This means that Annis was breastfeeding Marcus around the same time she was also nursing her own son, Richard. She also might have taught Marcus to read and write.

When he grew up, Marcus worked as a free servant in Philadelphia for Annis's daughter Julia and her husband, Dr. Benjamin Rush. Marcus was invaluable to the Rush family. He worked as an all-around handyman, caretaker, nurse, medical assistant and valued personal companion. The widowed Annis Stockton often inquired about Marcus in letters to her daughter. When Marcus nursed Dr. Rush back to health after a yellow fever scare in 1793, the doctor wrote, "I cannot tell you how much I owe to the fidelity and affection of our humble black friend. He has been a treasure to us in all our difficulties."

Benjamin Rush was also a signer of the Declaration of Independence. He was outspoken about the evils of slavery, despite having purchased a slave at the onset of the Revolutionary War. The man, named William Grubber, remained a slave to Rush even after the doctor joined the Pennsylvania Abolition Society. These mindboggling contradictions of enslavement, abolitionist sentiments and kindnesses are hard to reconcile, but they were common attitudes among slaveholding families.

Julia Rush's younger brother, Richard Stockton Jr. (known as the "Duke" for his imperious demeanor), referred to his inherited slaves as his "outdoor family"—a cruel joke describing the women and men who lived in simple outbuildings while they worked to support their rich masters and mistresses. Julia and Richard were probably the last Stockton generation to own slaves. By the 1840s, no enslaved people were recorded living at Morven. However, other African Americans, similar to Marcus Marsh, might have continued working for the Stockton family as servants or apprentices.

New Jersey's legislature passed An Act to Abolish Slavery in 1846. Not as accurate in its application as its name, the act redesignated slaves as "apprentices for life." Though the actual number of enslaved people continued to decrease, New Jersey would officially remain a slave state for another twenty years.

———

IN 1780, JOHN DENTON, a Princeton bookseller living on Nassau Street, advertised for a runaway named Caesar. Denton offered a substantial reward of $1,000 for the return of the man. Denton believed that Caesar had been "advised to go away," as if the enslaved man would need someone else's advice on how and why he would want to escape from bondage. The bookseller offered an additional $6,000 reward if it was found that a white person rendered this advice to Caesar. Adding bias to his perceived injury, Denton said he would pay only $500 if the advisor was a Black person.

Denton guessed Caesar would flee through Staten Island on the way to New York City and point north. Not one to waste good advertising dollars, Denton concluded his plea for the return of his slave with an offer to sell "sundry other kinds of merchandise," cattle, iron and salt.

———

THERE WERE ONLY TWELVE Princeton slaves in the 1840 U.S. Census. Albert B. Dod, a professor at the College of New Jersey, is listed as owning an unnamed female slave. He was hardly unique—the college's first nine presidents were all slaveholders.

Dod vigorously defended slavery on the grounds that Jesus never spoke about the practice in the Bible. Slaveholding was not illegal, he reasoned:

One Thousand Dollars Reward.
RAN AWAY,

From the fubfcriber, in Princeton, on Sunday evening the 12th inftant;

A NEGRO MAN, named Cæfar, about twenty-five years of age, about five feet eight inches high, marked with the fmall-pox; had on a blue camblet coat worn out at the elbows, a pair of new buckfkin breeches, ftraps without kneebuckles, old pumps with a hole in one of the toes or a new patch, a fmall felt hat lopt. Whoever apprehends the faid Negro and delivers him to me, fhall have the above reward, paid by   JOHN DENTON.

Princeton, Nov. 14, 1780.

P. S. There is good reafon to believe that he has been advifed to go away, any fubftantial evidence who will difcover the fact (if the plot be by a white perfon) on full conviction, fhall have a reward of Six Thoufand Dollars; if a black perfon, Five Hundred. As it is more than probable that there is more people goes to market to Staten-Ifland than ought; but if any perfon going there will pleafe to call on Mr. Cubberly and enquire of his negro man Cæfar who it was that advifed him to leave his mafter, and make a fufficient difcovery whereby the fubfcriber may receive fufficient damage, fhall have Ten Guineas or the exchange thereof in Continental money.

The fubfcriber has for fale, bar-iron, rock & fhore falt, fpelling-books and almanacks by the grofs or dozen as low as at Philadelphia, and fundry other kinds of merchandize. Alfo two yoke of fat oxen, with fome other fat cattle, to be fold at publick vendue on Saturday the 18th inftant, between the hours of eight and twelve o'clock in the forenoon, for ready money only; or at private fale, as may beft fuit the purchafer. Hard money will be moft agreeable—and no perfon to have the cattle to take them out of the ftate.   J. D.

Right: A Princeton bookseller named John Denton advertised for his runaway slave Caesar in a *New Jersey Gazette* in 1780. New Jersey Gazette *via Princeton & Slavery website.*

Below: The 1840 federal census lists a single woman slave owned by Princeton University professor Albert B. Dod. *1840 Federal Census.*

"Because masters may treat their slaves unjustly, is no more a valid argument against the lawfulness of slaveholding, than the abuse of parental authority… is an argument against the lawfulness of parental relation."

The professor's son Samuel Bayard Dod graduated from the college in 1857. A dozen years later, Samuel Dod established an endowed professorship in mathematics at the college to commemorate his father. In 1890, Albert Dod's sister Susan donated funds to build a campus dormitory named for her brother, the last Princeton instructor to own a slave. Although twenty-first-century Princeton students have urged the school's administration to change the name of university buildings associated with men who held racist beliefs, Dod Hall retains its commemorative title, as did the Woodrow Wilson School of Public and International Affairs, until June 2020.

Woodrow Wilson, born in Virginia before the Civil War, has strong associations with New Jersey. He was a graduate of Princeton University and became its president in 1902. He served as governor of New Jersey from 1911 to 1913, just before being elected president of the United States. All these fine credentials notwithstanding, Wilson is notorious for screening the blatantly racist *The Birth of a Nation* at the White House (though he afterward claimed that he did not approve of its content). Wilson appointed segregationist sympathizers to his cabinet, and his administration was accused of pursuing racist policies. Wilson once argued that "segregation was essential to the avoidance of friction" between the races.

D.W. Griffith was a New Jersey filmmaker and director of the infamous *The Birth of a Nation* in 1915. *Library of Congress.*

Four years after Princeton students raised their concerns about honoring the twenty-eighth president of the United States, the university's president conceded that it was time to make a change. "The university's board of trustees found that Wilson's 'racist thinking and policies make him an inappropriate namesake for a school or college whose scholars, students and alumni must stand firmly against racism in all its forms.'"

THE INTOLERANT LEANINGS OF the white elite students educated at Princeton persisted for years. An 1853 cartoon in a student newspaper called the *Nassau Rake* played on perceived common themes about free African Americans, particularly women. The illustrated street scene showed a pair of dandies whose dialog reflected an attitude not too far removed from how many slave masters thought of their female slaves—as sexual objects to be gazed on and then preyed on by white men of privilege.

T C BOYD

Scene from Real Life.—The Street.

P. and *A.*, (looking about as green as ever.)

P.—I say, A., these gals here ain't a darned bit pretty, are they?

A.—No, that they ain't; why down in Alabama, the gals are right down handsome. But they ain't so here.

P.—But I'll be darned if there ain't some right good looking niggar gals here, ain't they?

A.—Darned if they ain't.

A Princeton student newspaper called the *Nassau Rake* ridiculed undergraduates for their attitudes about African Americans in 1853. *Princeton & Slavery website.*

The *Rake*'s sophomore editors claimed their high-minded aim was "to censure the vices, to ridicule the follies, to exhibit the ignorance, and dissipate the impudence" of the other Princeton University classes. One wonders if the racial attitudes of the editors differed much from those of their intended targets. Or if the students being spoofed understood the barbs as irony, or if they viewed them as an accurate and funny reflection of widely held beliefs.

THE LIFE OF A former slave, James Collins, who earned his living selling peanuts to Princeton students, was one of persistence. Born in Maryland in 1816, Collins had escaped slavery by the time he was twenty-three. Though he was later circumspect about its details, he seems to have walked to Delaware, boarded a steamboat to Philadelphia and then took a train to Princeton. He was likely helped by the Underground Railroad as he tried to make his way farther north. Perhaps he ran out of friends and funds and decided Princeton was a safe enough place to begin a new life. Once settled in New Jersey, he arranged to have his wife, Phillis, and son, Thomas, join him.

Calling himself James C. Johnson, he supported his family by performing the kinds of mundane and unpleasant work not much removed from what slaves had always done. He cleaned students' rooms, kept their rooms warm by keeping their fires going and, most odious of all, emptied their outhouse latrine buckets. For this basic janitorial service, his educated "betters" cruelly called him "Jimmy Stink."

Johnson was eventually uncovered as a runaway by a Princeton student from Maryland who recognized him. Although prosecuted by his former owner under the Fugitive Slave Act of 1793, Johnson was saved from re-enslavement by a woman with family connections to the college. Theodosia Ann Mary Prevost bought Johnson's freedom for $500, though she does not appear to have been a particularly ardent abolitionist. The grateful Johnson worked for several years to repay her.

James Johnson was as resourceful as he was lucky. A fixture on campus, he sold students used clothing and furniture and hawked cold drinks, fruit, candy and other treats from a wheelbarrow. He assumed he had the exclusive right to this vending business, which earned him the sobriquet the "Peanut Man of Princeton." Johnson saved enough money to buy

Right: James Collins Johnson escaped Maryland slavery and established himself as a respected Princeton businessman during the nineteenth century. *Princeton & Slavery website.*

Below: Johnson was known as the "Peanut Man of Princeton" when he sold snacks to Princeton undergraduates. *Princeton & Slavery website.*

some property and marry several times. He was beloved by many on the Princeton campus, and perhaps more importantly, he became a revered figure in the local African American community.

The freeman James Collins Johnson knew his rights and was vocal about them. During a dispute with the college for allowing a white Civil War veteran to sell similar sundries, Johnson was told that the former serviceman had fought for the former slave's freedom. Insulted, Johnson angrily asserted, "I never got no free papers. Princeton College bought me; Princeton College owns me; and Princeton College has got to give me my living."

Though Johnson's diligence and longevity earned him living icon status on the Princeton campus and in town, some students still regarded him as an amusing mascot right until his death in 1902. A poem, "The Unsung Hero," from an 1890 edition of the *Tiger*, was attributed to "Prof. James Johnson, D.C.L." His faux academic credentials were explained to be "Dealer in Cool Lemonade."

9

SLAVE AUCTIONS OF CAMDEN; RUNAWAYS IN BURLINGTON

No more auction block for me
No more, no more
No more auction block for me
Many thousand gone.
—*Pete Seeger, "No More Auction Block"*

Burlington County, formed in 1694, is uniquely situated in New Jersey. With the Delaware River as its northwestern border, it spans the entire state all the way to Great Bay and the Atlantic Ocean. Swedes and Dutch settled along the Delaware before the English came to dominate the Jerseys.

New Jersey's founding document, *The Concession and Agreement of the Lords Proprietors*, firmly established slavery by offering colonists extra property called "head lands." Settlers were granted acreage per head, including seventy-five acres for each slave they brought along. The Quintipartite Deed, signed by William Penn and others, established East and West Jersey in 1676. Burlington's easternmost border was the dividing Keith Line between the two provinces. The town of Burlington was the county seat and the capital of West Jersey.

In 1704, Burlington passed An Act for Regulating Negro, Indian and Mallatto Slaves within This Province of New Jersey. Setting the tone for the denial of liberties and the harsh treatment of slaves, it prohibited anyone from buying or selling anything to slaves, required slaves to carry

Quaker meetinghouses like this one in Burlington were common in West Jersey. *The Century Magazine, published 1887.*

written travel passes, allowed for their arrest and whipping if they were found wandering too far from their masters' homes and detailed other severe punishments for slave crimes.

English Quakers from nearby Pennsylvania were among the earliest arrivals in Burlington. This might seem to explain West Jersey's historical inclination toward the abolition of slavery as opposed to the attitudes of East Jersey citizens. But as Princeton University's Geneva Smith has written:

> *West Jersey was less densely populated, since much of the land was sandy loam unsuited to agriculture. In part because of this lower labor demand, by 1800 only 507 slaves remained in the region. It is important to note these economic considerations to avoid overemphasizing the religious fervor or benevolence of antislavery Quakers. Economic motivations, religious convictions, and West Jersey's close ties with antislavery societies in Philadelphia all combined to create an environment hostile to slavery. In East Jersey, however, enslaved labor was widely used on large plantations and small farms, urban workshops, and especially at ports and docks.*

Although some Burlington Quakers still owned slaves during the eighteenth century, the "three great Quaker counties" of Burlington, Gloucester and Salem, home to almost a quarter of New Jersey's population, accounted for just 3 percent of its slaves by 1800.

JOHN ROGERS WAS BORN in March 1687, according to the Chesterfield Quaker Meeting records. His father's will stipulated that the thirteen-year-old John receive one year of schooling in preparation for an apprenticeship with a blacksmith. John must have been particularly diligent because he eventually acquired hundreds of acres in Springside, east of Burlington Town.

A modern field survey of the Rogers property showed a large verdant property surrounded by stately sycamores located on a brook just off a country road. Rogers built his large brick house there in 1718. His slaves tilled his fields, cultivated and harvested his fruit trees, milked his cows and slaughtered his pigs, pumped his well and performed the dozens of other

Slaveholder John Rogers built this brick house in Springside in 1718. *Library of Congress.*

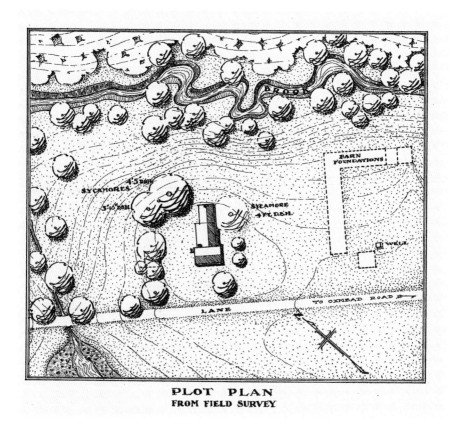

PLOT PLAN
FROM FIELD SURVEY

Rogers's slaves maintained his estate but lived in basic shelters like his animal barn. *Historic American Buildings Survey, 1937.*

mundane farm tasks for the wealthy Quaker. These slaves lived in basic quarters, perhaps even in the barn set off from the main house. Quakers like John Rogers had not yet come to the abolitionist beliefs still in early development by other West Jersey Friends.

⸺ ◦ ⸺

ACTIVIST QUAKERS, SUCH AS John Woolman of Mount Holly; Anthony Benezet and his student William Dillwyn of Philadelphia; Benjamin Lay of Abington, Pennsylvania; and Samuel Allison of Burlington, wrote fiery tracts that they read at meetinghouses throughout the Jerseys. These men became ever more strident, starting with advocating for better treatment for slaves and then urging their education and eventually proselytizing for the total abolishment of slavery. As a result, Quaker congregations sent petitions to the New Jersey Legislature for abolition of slavery. Still, the first state constitution of 1776 did not guarantee any "natural rights to people," nor did it free any New Jersey slaves.

Writing in his journal about a visit to the Chesterfield Meeting in 1753, Woolman noted that he'd been asked to assist in writing the will of a dying Quaker. The sick man wanted to leave his slaves to his children. Woolman felt conflicted and recalled, "As writing is a profitable employ and offending sober people was disagreeable to my inclination, I was straitened in my mind, but as I looked to

John Woolman was a fiery Quaker who traveled throughout New Jersey preaching abolition. *Wikimedia Commons.*

the Lord he inclined my heart to his testimony, and I told the man that I believed the practice of continuing slavery to this people was not right and had a scruple in my mind against doing writings of that kind: that though many in our Society kept them as slaves, still I was not easy to be concerned in it, and desired to be excused from going to write the will."

As much as he abhorred slavery, Woolman was a practical man too. He recognized how economically difficult it would be for Quakers to manumit their slaves immediately and unconditionally. Woolman strongly urged these Friends to treat their slaves more humanely. Though Woolman's fervor did not result in the abolition of slavery during his lifetime, he did influence the New Jersey Legislature enough to pass various acts restricting the slave trade.

John Woolman virtually predicted the Civil War one hundred years before that horrendous conflict fought over slavery. He wrote presciently that "if the white people retain a resolution to prefer their outward prospects of gain to all other considerations, and do not act conscientiously toward [slaves] as fellow-creatures, I believe that burden will grow heavier and heavier, until times change in a way disagreeable to us."

SLAVEHOLDERS WITH DIFFERENT RELIGIOUS beliefs viewed slavery in myriad ways. Quakers held slaves, and non-Quakers freed slaves. As always, human motivations and actions in seventeenth- and eighteenth-century New Jersey varied tremendously, sometimes in conformity with the law, and just as often, not.

The *History of Burlington County and Mercer Counties*, written in 1883, says little about slavery, intentionally trying to paint the brightest picture it could. Among the very few slaves mentioned is an Ishmael, owned by Isaac Budd, who lived near Pemberton. The slave's wife was unnamed, but we're told the man had two daughters, Imaleah and Beulah, who were eventually manumitted. A son called Freeborn (for that reason) lived to be 106 years old.

Ishmael was born in the 1750s. We can infer only a few things about how his family lived for over a century, mostly by what was written about his master, Isaac Budd. Budd was a farmer and ran a sawmill and a brick business. A contemporary map shows that the farmer was influential and prosperous; Budd Town was a decent-sized hamlet between Vincentown and Pemberton.

Ishmael and his son, Freeborn, were probably skilled in many trades. Besides milling and brick work, they would have acquired expertise in

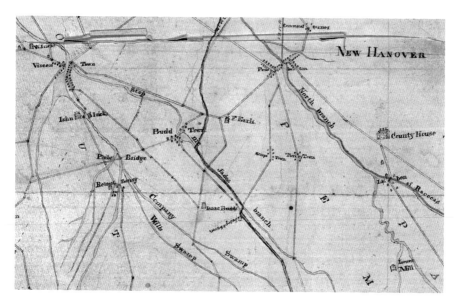

Budd Town in Burlington County was named for slaveholder Isaac Budd. *Burlington County Map, 1849.*

important farming operations such as blacksmithing, carpentry and animal husbandry. Budd, a Methodist, had a lot of slaves working on his plantation. Few are named, and the others were deemed too inconsequential to merit mention.

Isaac Budd owned at least three other slaves. He registered a male, Edwards Eairs, born on August 13, 1804. Two and a half years later, Budd notified the Burlington County Courthouse that "George Eayres [*sic*]" was born to his slave Lydia Eayres, possibly Edward's mother too. No father is noted in either certificate. These might be the only records indicating these three people ever existed.

———

CHARLES READ WAS A white man who moved to Burlington from Philadelphia around 1739. He immersed himself in local politics, became a court clerk and a customs collector and held various other official provincial roles. Read was an entrepreneur with interests in real estate, agriculture and lumbering. He opened a number of iron forges during the 1760s. He was an acquaintance of the Schuylers, the slaveholding copper mining family of Bergen County.

Read used both indentured servants and slaves to run his furnaces at Atsion, opened in 1765. The next year, he established furnaces at Batsto on the Mullica River, at Aetna (or New Etna) and at Taunton. These furnaces sat on almost ten thousand acres of crucial timber land. Read's slaves did the demanding work of mining the abundant bog iron ore, cutting trees and burning the wood for charcoal to fuel the insatiable furnaces producing pig iron.

The Pine Barrens lands of Charles Read were particularly well suited to his commercial endeavors—the bog ore came from the area's numerous waterways and rivers. Though they may not have been as imposing as Pine Brook, which Lewis Morris dammed at Tinton Falls in Monmouth County, the Burlington streams on Read's properties provided enough power for the water wheels and gears his slaves needed for making colonial iron.

These slaves became expert artisans as they forged pots, kettles and stoves and designed elaborate fireplace backings or stove plates. In turn, these skills increased their resale value. A typical ad at the time read, "Six Negro Slaves to hire out or sell, who are good Forgemen, and understand the making of Iron well." The output from these and other Jersey furnaces powered by slave labor was vital to the rebel colonials during the Revolutionary War.

Fireplace backings like this one from Charles Read's Aetna Furnace were the handicraft of his highly skilled slaves. *Metropolitan Museum of Art (NY) catalog*

Charles Read was also interested in agriculture and wrote an extensive series of notes on farming. He gave details of farm structures and farm implements and plans for the construction of barracks, cow sheds, fences, gates and other essential farm necessities. He was particularly keen on horse breeding, managing cattle to produce dairy products and handling pigs for pork. Read listed the most effective dates for planting, blossoming and ripening various vegetable crops he cultivated. He wanted to grow fruit trees and wrote, "A peach orchard was a scheme I have long intended to putt [*sic*] in execution."

The intricate descriptions of agricultural methods were, no doubt, the result of Charles Read's direct observation of what his hardworking slaves accomplished. Of course, they received neither mention nor credit.

WILLIAM BOEN WAS BORN into slavery in 1735 as the chattel property of Moses Haines of Westhampton. Like other eighteenth-century Quakers who owned slaves, Haines took Boen with him to the Mount Holly Meeting. Boen was relegated to the last pew, indicative of his outsider status.

In a book about his life, Boen was described as:

> *Being a slave from his birth, he had very little opportunity of acquiring useful learning; yet by his own industry and care, he succeeded in learning to read and write. His mind became seriously impressed while very young, and he was induced in early life, to attend to the monitions of light and life in his own mind, being convinced from what he felt within him, of the existence of a Supreme Being; and also of the manner of his visiting the children of men, by the inward peace which he felt upon a faithful performance of what he thus apprehended to be his duty.*

William Boen was twenty-eight years old when he informed the Mount Holly Meeting that he wanted to exchange wedding vows with a former slave named Dinah. The woman, sometimes called Dido, worked for the Joseph Burr family in Chesterfield.

The Quakers objected because Boen, "having entered into marriage engagements with a woman in the neighbourhood, but [was] not being, at that time, a member of our society." The adamant abolitionist John Woolman intervened on July 3, 1763, and saw to it that the meeting "had a number of persons convened where they [William and Dido] were married after the manner of our Society, and a certificate to that effect, furnished by those present."

William Boen was eventually manumitted. Nonetheless, and primarily because of his color, Boen had to wait another fifty years before he was granted official Society of Friends membership—this despite living what everyone recognized as an exemplary life.

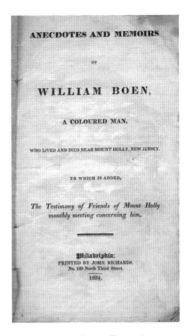

ANECDOTES AND MEMOIRS

OF

WILLIAM BOEN,

A COLOURED MAN,

WHO LIVED AND DIED NEAR MOUNT HOLLY, NEW JERSEY.

TO WHICH IS ADDED,

The Testimony of Friends of Mount Holly monthly meeting concerning him.

Philadelphia:
PRINTED BY JOHN RICHARDS,
No. 129 North Third Street.
1834.

Slave William Boen (Bowen) was denied the right to marry at the Mount Holly Friends Meeting until John Woolman intervened. Anecdotes and Memoirs of William Boen, *1834.*

Another account about Boen, written sixty years after his death in 1824, refers to him as William Bowen, who was "worthy of mention among the colored people." This paternalistic description was an attempt to make New Jersey slavery palatable and benign to a white majority's belief in its own benevolence.

Bowen "learned the trade of a wool-comber, and in his later years earned a living at that business. His prejudices in regard to slavery were strong.... He would neither eat, drink, or wear anything manufactured or that came through the servitude of his race. He was a Christian in every sense of the word." All of this might be accurate about William Bowen/Boen, but this later version minimized the man's lifelong attempt for acceptance into the Quaker community.

In his memoirs, written just before he died, Boen himself revealed an unwavering hope despite his many setbacks. He was quoted, saying, "He had thought he was alone with regard to his testimony against slavery... [but] he believed it would grow and increase among Friends."

THIRD-GENERATION SLAVEHOLDER WILLIAM EVANS descended from the original Welsh Quakers who settled Burlington County. When it came to disciplining his bondmen, Evans revealed the capriciousness of slaveholders in a February 1778 newspaper advertisement:

> *To be sold, For no fault but a saucy tongue, for which he is now in the Burlington gaol.*
> *A negro man about 39 years of age. He is a compleat farmer, honest and sober. For further particulars enquire of the subscriber in Evesham, Burlington county. William Evans*

Apparently, even though the unnamed slave had valuable skills and desirable personal characteristics, he was being sold because he was irreverent and probably talked back to Evans after some mistreatment. White masters could brook no challenge to their authority, and Evans had the slave jailed because of his impudence.

IN THE FIRST DECADE or so of the eighteenth century, Daniel Cooper obtained a Camden County license to operate a ferry on the Delaware River. His boats navigated between Cooper's Point (Camden) and Philadelphia. Philadelphia Quakers, in a 1761 attempt to thwart slave dealers, successfully lobbied the local government to impose import duties on slaves. Because New Jersey had no such taxes, slave traders simply moved across the river to Cooper's Ferry, then run by Benjamin Cooper, Daniel's son and a Quaker.

By May of the next year, slaves were being sold at auction at Cooper's Ferry. A Philadelphia newspaper announcement revealed the contemporary callous marketing of human beings:

> *Just imported from the River Gambia in the Schooner* Sally, *Bernard Badger, Master, and to be sold at the Upper Ferry (called Benjamin Cooper's Ferry), opposite to this City, a parcel of likely Men and Women Slaves, with some Boys and Girls of different Ages. Attendance will be given from the hours of nine to twelve o'clock in the Morning, and from three to six in the Afternoon, by W. Coxe, S. Oldman, and Company.*

Camden was originally the site of Cooper's Ferry, where West Jersey slave auctions were held. *Historical Society of Pennsylvania.*

N.B. It is generally allowed that the Gambian Slaves are much more robust and tractable than any other slaves from the Coast of Guinea, and more Capable of undergoing the Severity of the Winter Seasons in the North-American Colonies, which occasions their being Vastly more esteemed and coveted in this Province and those to the Northward, than any other Slaves whatsoever.

Quakers were no different from other businessmen in pursuing profits by operating slave auctions at Delaware River ferry terminals. Conveniently, these riverside stops offered water deep enough to accommodate slave ships coming directly from Africa. Conditions about these ships were unimaginably horrible. An 1829 report about one of them offered these still-stunning details:

The ship had been at sea for 17 days with 500 kidnapped Africans onboard. Fifty-five had already been thrown overboard. The Africans were crowded below the main deck. Each deck was only 3 feet 3 inches high.

165

They were packed together so tight that they were sitting up between one another's legs, everyone completely nude…no possibility of their lying down or at all changing their position.

Each had been branded with the red hot iron on their breast or arm. Many were children, little girls, and little boys. The heat of these horrid places was so great and the odor so offensive that it was quite impossible to enter them, even if there had been room. These people, these human beings, sat in their own vomit, urine and feces, and that of others. If another person sat between your legs, their bowels emptied out on you.

Many of the enslaved, sick or driven mad, were thrown overboard. There was so much human flesh going over the side of those ships that sharks learned to trail them.

Of four generations of Cooper slaveholders, Marmaduke Cooper might have held more than any in his family. No fewer than fourteen enslaved Africans tended to his four-hundred-acre plantation. In 2017, Camden County Historical Society research disclosed these details:

While the auctions held at three different ferries in Camden appear to be limited to the 1760s, these sales likely introduced upwards of 500 new slaves to west New Jersey and eastern Pennsylvania. The regular movement of slave vessels up the Delaware River began in the 1750s, arriving at docks along the Philadelphia shore. Between 1757 and 1766, 1,300 African slaves reportedly disembarked from the Guinea ships. In addition to the newly arrived Africans, the Cooper ferries served as a venue for selling previously owned single slaves and small groups of those held in bondage.

Quaker activist John Woolman was alarmed at these New Jersey slave auctions as early as 1762. In his influential *Considerations on the Keeping of Negroes,* he tried to convince slaveholders to adopt his abolitionist positions by appealing to their sense of self-respect. He wrote that their attitudes would affect their own humanity:

Placing on men the ignominious title SLAVE, dressing them in uncomely garments, keeping them to servile labor, in which they are often dirty, tends gradually to fix a notion in the mind, that they are a sort of people below us in nature, and leads us to consider them as such in all our conclusions about them. And, moreover, a person which in our esteem is mean and contemptible, if their language or behavior toward us is unseemly or

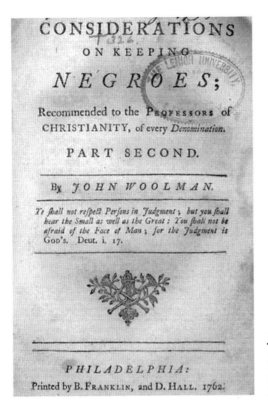

John Woolman's *Considerations on Keeping Negroes* was printed by Benjamin Franklin in 1762. Considerations on Keeping Negroes, *1762*.

disrespectful, it excites wrath more powerfully than the like conduct in one we accounted our equal or superior; and where this happens to be the case, it disqualifies for candid judgment; for it is unfit for a person to sit as judge in a case where his own personal resentments are stirred up; and, as members of society in a well framed government, we are mutually dependent. Present interest incites to duty, and makes each man attentive to the convenience of others; but he whose will is a law to others, and can enforce obedience by punishment; he whose wants are supplied without feeling any obligation to make equal returns to his benefactor, his irregular appetites find an open field for motion, and he is in danger of growing hard, and inattentive to their convenience who labor for his support; and so loses that disposition, in which alone men are fit to govern.

THE HUGG FAMILY FROM Ireland were original settlers of Camden County. Around 1683, John Hugg, a Quaker, bought five hundred acres near the Delaware River. Hugg was also a slaveholder and is recorded as selling "a negro boy" named Sambo in 1709. Some Hugg slave descendants who were manumitted chose to remain on their former master's property and renamed it to remind them of their African heritage. The Still family were among the freed Blacks who lived in Guinea Town for a while in the early nineteenth century. They traced their roots to a royal prince in Guinea.

Levin Still was born enslaved on a Maryland plantation around 1775. Excited by the possibilities of New Jersey's Gradual Abolition Act of 1804, he bought his freedom and moved north, temporarily leaving his wife, Charity, with their four young children. Levin hoped to find work that would allow him to save enough money to buy his family's freedom.

Not content to wait for what might be years, Charity Still engineered her own escape but was soon recaptured. Returned to her Chesapeake Bay owner, she took off again, traveling north with her children. While Charity was at church one day, her two boys were kidnapped and then sold and sent deep into Kentucky slave territory.

Distraught but with little recourse or resources to find their lost sons, Charity and Levin settled into a new life in New Jersey, where they raised a large family. Several of their eighteen children rose to prominence.

James Still was born in Washington Township, Burlington County, in 1812. Hired out by his father as an indentured servant when he was a teenager, James studied Native American herbal remedies. He concocted a cough balm from natural ingredients that was so successful he became one of the wealthiest men in southwest Jersey. He purchased substantial real estate holdings in Medford Township.

Still was threatened with legal action by the established medical community for daring to help patients, as if he were an actual trained physician. With palpable jealousy, the Medical Society of New Jersey scurrilously called him "an Ethiopian enjoying a large and lucrative practice, guided...solely by inspiration." Nonetheless, by the time he died in 1885, James Still was highly regarded as the "Doctor of the Pines" by both Black and white patients.

James's younger brother by nine years, William Still, became quite famous in his own right. Working in Philadelphia, William was part of a group performing the dangerous work of relocating runaway slaves. He became celebrated as the "Father of the Underground Railroad," a reputation enhanced by the popularity of his self-penned book of 1872, *The Underground Railroad*.

William Still was obviously inspired by the powerful example of his parents' flight from slavery. As chairman of the Pennsylvania Anti-Slavery Society, he and his compatriots helped hundreds of people reach freedom in Upstate New York and Canada in the years before the Civil War, perhaps as many as eight hundred runaways. As real as William Still's heroic endeavors were, many other Black men and women who assisted runaways might be considered cofounders of the UGRR. Not least among them was Harriet Tubman (see chapter 10).

As noteworthy as James and William Still were, their older brother Peter's life exceeded theirs for its poignant drama. Peter and Levin Jr. were the two Still sons abducted in 1810 before they could reach freedom in New Jersey. They were six and eight years old at the time. After laboring in Kentucky for thirteen hard years in a brick factory and in cotton fields, the brothers were sold again, this time to separate families in Alabama. When Levin Jr. died in 1831, Peter despaired of ever seeing any of his family again. Yet against what seemed insurmountable odds, he never gave up hope.

In 1826, Peter married a slave woman named Lavinia "Vina" Sisson from a nearby plantation. Around 1850, Peter was sold yet again for $500. His new owners allowed him to earn his own money, hiring him out as a handyman. Peter managed to buy his own freedom by reimbursing his sympathetic owners his $500 purchase price. He planned to go north, reconnect with his family of origin and then return to secure his Alabama family's freedom.

PETER STILL,
THE KIDNAPPED AND RANSOMED.

Kidnapped when he was six years old, Peter Still was reunited with his siblings and mother in New Jersey after forty years of slavery. *Public domain.*

Arriving in Cincinnati, Peter spent a fearful night in a boardinghouse listening for the ubiquitous slave catchers he was sure would find him. The next morning, he went to meet with abolitionists at the Pennsylvania Anti-Slavery Society. During a conversation about his life's wanderings, Peter was informed by the "clerk" he was speaking with that they were probably brothers. William Still was convinced by the details of Peter's story, but because it seemed so unlikely, Peter was skeptical and suspicious that he was being tricked, as he had been so often. The two men had never met; William was born in New Jersey a decade after Peter and Levin Jr. had been sold into slavery. More startling to Peter, he was told that his mother was still alive and living just across the Delaware River in New Jersey, a place he had never heard of.

Brought to meet two sisters he had also not known, Peter's doubts and fears slowly subsided after they told him they "saw in him a striking likeness to both their parents." Kitty and Mary accompanied Peter to the Medford home of yet another of his newfound siblings, Dr. James Still. The next morning, Peter Still took the eight-mile trip to his eighty-year-old mother's home. Forty years after she had last seen him, Charity Still's bewildered first reaction was to walk "into the next room, where she knelt in prayer." Then, as Peter related in a book of his recollections, "the long-lost son was blest. He clasped his mother to his warm, full heart, and joyful tears stole down his dusky cheeks."

Fortified by this happy turn of events in his life, Peter Still was determined to liberate his wife and three children from Alabama. He returned to Cincinnati, had his previous owners give him a slave pass and, risking everything, went back to Tuscumbia. He concocted a plan with an abolitionist who agreed to bring Vina Still and the children north. But fate thwarted Peter Still once again when Vina was apprehended in Indiana and sent back south.

Peter Still, as resolute as ever, spent the next four years touring the country and speaking out about his family's plight. He finally raised the $4,000 his family's owners demanded. Vina and their children, Peter, Levin and Catharine, finally rejoined Peter in 1855. The family started their new life together in Burlington fifty years after Peter Still's parents had done the same.

NEW JERSEY'S RELATIVELY SMALL size and its location between the important population centers of Philadelphia and New York City made it a natural gateway for southern slaves escaping in the nineteenth century. Existing free Black communities in southwest Jersey were supportive. Conductors guided passengers on the UGRR routes once they traversed the Delaware River. Sympathetic station masters hosted safe houses along the way to New York.

More than one route through Burlington County earned it the title of the "Cradle of Emancipation." Seton Hall University history professor Larry A. Greene described them this way: "A network of routes, safe houses, and

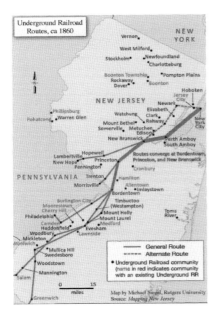

Underground Railroad routes crisscrossed New Jersey, leading escaped slaves to New York. *Rutgers University.*

abolitionist sympathizers acting as conductors formed the Underground Railroad (UGRR). The state had three main routes: from Camden to Burlington, following the Delaware River; from Salem through Woodbury, Mount Laurel, and Burlington to Princeton; and through Greenwich, with stations at Swedesboro, Mount Holly, and Burlington directing the runaways to the Camden route."

Wilbur Henry Siebert researched and described these routes in 1898. There were myriad tributaries to the established escape paths in response to the activities of pursuing slave catchers, the time of year and seasonal weather, among other factors.

Even when provided with food, clothing and temporary housing, runaway slaves never felt truly safe and much less so after the Fugitive Slave Act of 1850 was passed by the federal government. Sometimes, the runaways were hidden in remodeled chimneys with concealed trapdoors, so-called body-hiding boxes. Or they wedged themselves behind false walls. There was little room in these tight enclosures. Often the escapees would stand upright for hours as they waited for their hosts to bring food and water. They listened for a signal to take a much-needed bathroom break. A fireplace might radiate minimal heat in winter. Hot and humid summer conditions were unbearable in the confined spaces, with only basic ventilation provided by peepholes. Yet runaways were more than willing to spend days and nights under stifling conditions before moving on to the next safe house and then another on the way north.

At even greater risk of exposure were the African Americans who were enthusiastic UGRR conductors and stationmasters. One such man was Peter Mott, born enslaved in Delaware in 1810 before fleeing north in his early twenties. His wife, Elizabeth Ann Thomas, was probably already emancipated when they married in 1833.

The Motts settled in the free Black community of Snow Hill in Camden County. The town, also called Free Haven, was developed around 1838

VOL. III. No. VII.   JULY, 1837.   WHOLE No. 31.

This picture of a poor fugitive is from one of the stereotype cuts manufactured in this city for the southern market, and used on handbills offering rewards for runaway slaves.

Runaway slaves on the Underground Railroad carried little with them on their way to freedom. *Public domain.*

by a white abolitionist named Ralph Smith, an official in a Philadelphia antislavery organization. The town's earliest roots might date to colonial times, when it was a settlement of free people of color.

Peter Mott became an ordained African Methodist Episcopal (AME) minister and was the pastor of the Mount Pisgah AME Church. He purchased several parcels of land during the 1840s and built a house in what is now Lawnside, New Jersey. The two-story Mott home is preserved today and celebrated as an important station on the UGRR, unique in that it was owned by African Americans.

Free Blacks like the Motts were at double jeopardy for their activities. Not only were they obvious suspects who might harbor escaped slaves, but they themselves could also be targets of unscrupulous slave catchers empowered by the Fugitive Slave Act. If caught sheltering slaves, free Blacks risked being shackled and sent south alongside recaptured men and women. The slave catchers were bounty hunters interested in profits, with little regard for legality. The courageous Peter Mott died in 1881, after somehow surviving years of danger.

Lawnside Historical Society president Linda Shockley, referencing the oral histories of runaway slaves, said, "Peter [Mott] carried the freedom seekers in his wagon to the Friends in Haddonfield and Moorestown….When the Motts were hiding runaway slaves, the women in the community would help Eliza by cooking extra food." Such was the dedication of successful escaped slaves to pass along their good fortune to others.

10

THE UNDERGROUND RAILROAD IN SALEM AND CAPE MAY COUNTIES

One more river to cross, one more mountain to climb,
One more valley that I gotta go through
Leavin' all my troubles behind.
One more battle with the Devil and I know he'll understand.
— Bud Chambers, "One More River to Cross"

In 1801, New Jersey slave catchers placed a newspaper notification about one of their captives: "Jim, runaway 18 month ago, and says when away, that he lived in Jersey, opposite New-Castle." These bounty hunters were only interested in financial rewards, but they also unknowingly enabled other slaves to effect successful escapes.

If Jim's owner saw the ad and had his human "property" returned from Salem County, all was not lost for Jim and his contemporary enslaved companions. Jim had acquired invaluable knowledge. He could share stories about friendly abolitionists, safe routes on the Underground Railroad, which rivers and streams were easiest to cross and more—almost an oral prospectus for the UGRR. As disappointing as failures were, at the same time, they served as powerful incentives for enslaved men and women to think "they can't catch us all; some of us will surely make it to freedom." Many did.

UGRR conductor William Still was in frequent contact with one of the most important of southern New Jersey UGRR station masters, Abigail Goodwin. She was dismissed from the Salem Friends Meeting for being too radical. She and her sister, Elizabeth, were actively engaged in helping runaways from the 1830s through the Civil War years. They solicited food, clothing and money from Quaker abolitionists as more and more slaves came through New Jersey from Delaware, Maryland and Virginia. The Goodwin sisters cofounded the Female Benevolent Society of Salem.

A man named Sam was one of the runaways who made his way to the Goodwin house. William Still wrote about Sam's unique story in his definitive *The Underground Railroad: A Record of Facts, Authentic Narratives, Letters, Etc.* Sam was "thirty one years of age, a man of medium size, and about as purely colored, as could readily be found, with a full share of self-esteem and pluck."

ABIGAIL GOODWIN.
See p. 617.

Abigail Goodwin and her sister were Quaker station masters of the Underground Railroad in Salem. The Underground Railroad: A Record of Facts, Authentic Narratives, Letters, Etc., *1872.*

With virtually no training from his Norfolk, Virginia master, Dr. Martin, Sam nonetheless grew skilled in dental work. He was his owner's bookkeeper, as well, completely uncompensated for any of this highly specialized work, of course. But Sam was also a UGRR agent. Suspecting he was soon to be found out in 1855, Sam got on a schooner bound for Philadelphia. He planned to send for his wife, Edna, and daughter, Elizabeth, once he obtained his freedom.

Dropped off unexpectedly at a lower Delaware Bay port, Sam and some others were told they'd have to make it to the City of Brotherly Love on their own. William Still recounted what happened next: "In making their way in the direction of their destined haven, they reached Salem, New Jersey, where they were discovered to be strangers and fugitives, and were directed to Abigail Goodwin, a Quaker lady, an abolitionist, long noted for her devotion to the cause of freedom, and one of the most liberal and faithful friends of the Vigilance Committee of Philadelphia."

Abigail Goodwin initially doubted Sam's story—a slave dentist?—but was reassured when Still wrote confirming letters to her. Sam finally made it to New Bedford, Massachusetts, where he came to be known as Dr. Thomas Bayne, DDS.

William Still touchingly memorialized station master Abigail Goodwin: "She worked for the slave as a mother would work for her children....Abigail Goodwin was one of the rare, true friends to the Underground Rail Road, whose labors entitle her name to be mentioned in terms of very high praise."

THE MOST FAMOUS OF all UGRR conductors is Harriet Tubman. She earned the sobriquet "Moses" because she led so many of her people out of exile to their eventual freedom. Barely five feet tall, this dynamic woman exuded bravery, grit and determination, exceeding the zeal of most people involved in the abolition movement.

So many books and articles have been written about her and so many films produced (including the 2019 movie *Harriet*) that it can be a challenge to remember she was a living, breathing woman, not simply a heroic archetype. But real she was, and successful beyond what anyone of her time could have expected.

Born around 1820 in Maryland, Araminta Ross's early life as a slave included the usual assortment of household domestic work and farm field labors. She was not unacquainted with brutality either. When an overseer threw a heavy weight at the teenage Araminta when she tried to protect another slave, the resulting head injury gave her headaches for the rest of her life, a constant reminder of her slave origins and an inspiration for her work to help others escape their demeaning circumstances.

In her mid-twenties, Araminta adopted her mother's first name and her husband, John's, last to become Harriet Tubman. In 1849, convinced she would be sold, she escaped to Philadelphia. With the confidence of the newly self-liberated and leveraging her contacts with William Still and other UGRR workers, Harriett made repetitive trips back to Maryland, leading her sister, her brother and other slaves north.

On a return to look for her husband, John, she was disappointed to find that he had remarried. Overcoming this personal loss, Harriet Tubman led others away. After the Fugitive Slave Act was passed in 1850, Tubman reacted with greater urgency as she recognized the increased peril. She stepped up her plans to help more people escape slavery.

Who could suspect the diminutive Tubman of the skill and daring necessary for a UGRR conductor? When she worked as a maid and a cook in Cape May, few casual observers would think it likely that a houseworker had the audacious bravery to travel back and forth over the Delaware River at great personal hazard.

Great leaders distinguish themselves by humbly acknowledging they don't know everything. Harriet Tubman gathered information from many other UGRR associates in Cape May and Philadelphia. She learned about the

Harriet Tubman is the most famous Underground Railroad conductor of all. *Public domain.*

best escape routes, the most reliable small boat operators, the safest towns and the most sympathetic contacts. She took good advice from anyone, Black or white, and coordinated with experienced abolitionists from southern New Jersey towns like Springtown, Marshalltown, Snow Hill and Haddonfield.

Harriet Tubman took nearly twenty excursions back and forth between slave country and New Jersey. She helped her seventy-year-old parents escape. She armed herself and was unafraid to threaten nervous and wavering runaways with a gun—"You'll be free or die." Despite a $40,000 reward for her capture, Harriet was never caught, even boasting that she never lost a UGRR passenger.

During the Civil War, Tubman was a Union cook, nurse, scout, soldier and spy. She made forays into Confederate-held territory, disguising herself in the role of an inconsequential slave woman but collecting information about rebel troop movements, supply lines and the like. The actual number of people she saw to freedom was substantial, although scholars have lately disputed the widely quoted estimate of Tubman's three hundred UGRR passengers.

Renowned abolitionist figures such as Frederick Douglass and John Brown were in awe of Harriet Tubman. Douglass wrote reverently to her after the war: "Excepting John Brown—of sacred memory—I know of no one who has willingly encountered more perils and hardships to serve our enslaved people than you have. Much that you have done would seem improbable to those who do not know you as I know you. It is to me a great pleasure and a great privilege to bear testimony to your character and your works, and to say to those to whom you may come, that I regard you in every way truthful and trustworthy."

When the Civil War was over and slavery permanently abolished by the Thirteenth Amendment, Tubman did not rest on her triumphs. She joined with prominent suffragettes to lobby for women's rights, looked after her aging parents and wrote an autobiography. She married a former slave and Union soldier, Nelson Davis. They resided in Auburn, New York, and adopted a daughter. After Davis died, Harriet spent years fighting for, and eventually winning, a widow's military pension—eight dollars per month. Her own military service was also recognized. She received twenty dollars per month beginning in 1899.

The indefatigable Harriet Tubman opened and ran the Home for Aged Negroes, into which she herself moved, penniless, toward the end of her life. This most remarkable of women died in 1913. She was buried at Fort Hill Cemetery in Auburn with military honors.

Tubman continued to work for the abolitionist movement and other social causes until her death in 1913. *Public domain.*

Harriet Tubman might never have read these words of Dr. James Still's, but she certainly embodied their spirit: "My colored friends, should you conduct yourselves on true moral principles, not gaudy in manners nor boisterous in talk, your ways calm and decisive, your word so sacred that 'tis never violated, your promises fulfilled, your debts paid, modest in all things and meddlesome in none, you shall find the monster Prejudice only a thing to be talked about. Merit alone will promote you to respect."

Yet with such a distinguished lifetime of accomplishments, as of this writing, the effort to replace Andrew Jackson's image on the United States twenty-dollar bill with Harriet Tubman's picture is stalled. Although the United States Treasury Department first announced this small gesture to honor her in 2016, a retrogressive Washington, D.C. bureaucracy has not budged. Harriet Tubman and her legacy have one more river to cross.

BIBLIOGRAPHY

Adelberg, Michael. *The Sandy Hook Lighthouse During the American Revolution.* *Keeper's Log* (Spring 1995): 10–15.

Ambuske, Jim, and Jeanette Patrick, eds. "William (Billy) Lee." Digital Encyclopedia of George Washington. https://www.mountvernon.org.

American Iron and Steel Association. *The Bulletin of the American Iron and Steel Association.* Philadelphia: Association, 1886. https://books.google.com/books?id=07Y2AQAAMAAJ.

Armstrong, Edward, ed. *Correspondence Between William Penn and James Logan and Others, 1700–1750.* Philadelphia: J.B. Lippincott & Co., 1870.

Asbury Park Press, various dates.

Axel-Lute, Paul. "The Law of Slavery in New Jersey: An Annotated Bibliography." New Jersey Digital Legal Library. Updated April 2013. http://njlegallib.rutgers.edu.

Balmer, Randall Herbert, and John R. Fitzmier. *The Presbyterians.* Westport, CT: Greenwood Press, 1993.

Barber, John W., and Henry Howe. *Historical Collections of the State of New Jersey.* New York: S. Tuttle, 1846.

Barnett, Robert L. *Lucy Harris-Jackson (c1780–c1875): The End of Slavery, and the Last People Enslaved in South Jersey.* Atlantic County Historical Society Yearbook. October 2007.

Bayonne Centennial Committee. *Bayonne Centennial Historical Revue.* Bayonne, NJ: Progress Printing Co., 1961.

Beekman, George C. *Early Dutch Settlers of Monmouth County, New Jersey.* Freehold, NJ: Moreau Bros., 1901.

Bibko, Julia. "The American Revolution and the Black Loyalist Exodus." *History: A Journal of Student Research* 1 (December 2016): 58–73. https://digitalcommons.brockport.edu.

Bilby, Joseph G. *New Jersey, A Military History*. Yardley, PA: Westholme Publishing, 2017.

Bisbee, Henry H., and Rebecca Bisbee Colesar, eds. *The Burlington Town Book, 1694–1785*. Burlington, NJ: Henry H. Bisbee, 1975.

Block, Kristen. *Ordinary Lives in the Early Caribbean, Religion, Colonial Competition, and the Politics of Profit*. Athens: University of Georgia Press, 2012.

Blow, Charles W. "Yes, Even George Washington." *New York Times*, June 28, 2020.

Boen, William. *Anecdotes and Memoirs of William Boen, a Coloured Man, Who Lived and Died Near Mount Holly, New Jersey*. Philadelphia: John Richards, 1834.

Bolton, Robert. *History of the County of Westchester, from Its First Settlement to the Present Times*. New York: Alexander S. Gould, 1848.

Brissot de Warville, J.P. *New Travels in the United States of America. Performed in 1788*. Dublin, Ireland: W. Corbet, 1792.

Brodhead, John Romeyn. *Documents Relative to the Colonial History of the State of New York; Procured in Holland, England and France*. Albany, NY: Weed, Parsons and Co., 1856.

Brown, T. Robins, and Schuyler Warmflash. *The Architecture of Bergen County, New Jersey: The Colonial Period to the Twentieth Century*. New Brunswick, NJ: Rutgers University Press, 2001.

Buck, Elaine, and Beverly Mills. *If These Stones Could Talk: African American Presence in the Hopewell Valley, Sourland Mountain, and Surrounding Regions of New Jersey*. Lambertville, NJ: Wild River Books, 2018.

Burr, Nelson R. *A Narrative and Descriptive Bibliography of New Jersey*. New York: D. Van Nostrand Co., 1964.

Cadbury, Henry. "Negro Membership in the Society of Friends." *Journal of Negro History* 21 (1936): 151–213. http://www.qhpress.org.

Carrington, Wirt Johnson. *A History of Halifax County (Virginia)*. Richmond, VA: Appeals Press, 1924.

Chambers, Theodore Frelinghuysen. *The Early Germans of New Jersey: Their History, Churches, and Genealogies*. Dover, NJ: Dover Printing Co., 1895.

Christ Church, Shrewsbury, New Jersey, Christ Church databases.

Clayton, W. Woodford, and Nelson William. *History of Bergen and Passaic Counties New Jersey, with Biographical Sketches of Many of Its Pioneers and Prominent Men*. Philadelphia: Everts & Peck, 1882.

Cooley, Henry Scofield. *A Study of Slavery in New Jersey*. Baltimore, MD: Johns Hopkins Press, 1896.

Cornish, Samuel E., and Theodore S. Wright. *The Colonization Scheme Considered, in Its Rejection by the Colored People*. Newark, NJ: Aaron Guest, 1840.

De Jong, Gerald Francis. *The Dutch Reformed Church and Negro Slavery in Colonial America*. Church History. N.p., 1971.

Denton, Daniel. *A Brief Description of New-York: Formerly Called New-Netherlands*. London: Printed for John Hancock, 1670.

Descendants of the Signers of the Declaration of Independence. "Richard Stockton." December 11, 2011. https://www.dsdi1776.com.

Donnan, Elizabeth, ed. *Documents Illustrative of the History of the Slave Trade to America, 1883–1955*. Washington, D.C.: Carnegie Institution of Washington, 1931.

Dorwart, Jeffrey M. *Cape May County, New Jersey, the Making of an American Resort Community*. New Brunswick, NJ: Rutgers University Press, 1992.

Dunbar, Erica Armstrong. *Never Caught: The Washingtons' Relentless Pursuit of Their Runaway Slave, Ona Judge*. New York: Simon and Schuster, 2017.

Dunlap, William. *A History of the Rise and Progress of the Arts of Design in the United States*. Vol. 1. New York: George P. Scott and Co., 1834.

Eaton, Harriet Phillips. *Jersey City and Its Historic Sites*. Jersey City, NJ: Woman's Club of Jersey City, 1899.

Edsall, Preston W., ed. *Journal of the Courts of Common Right and Chancery of East New Jersey, 1683–1702*. Philadelphia: American Legal History Society, 1937.

Ellis, Clifton, and Rebecca Ginsburg, eds. *Slavery in the City: Architecture and Landscapes of Urban Slavery in North America*. Charlottesville: University of Virginia Press, 2017.

Ellis, Franklin. *History of Monmouth County, New Jersey*. Philadelphia: R.T. Peck & Co., 1885.

Federal Writers' Project of the Work Projects Administration. *New Jersey: A Guide to Its Present and Past*. New York: Viking Press, 1939.

Finkelman, Paul, ed. *Encyclopedia of African American History, 1619–1895*. New York: Oxford University Press, 2006.

Freeman's Journal or North-American Intelligencer (Philadelphia), various dates.

Frey, Sylvia R. *Water from the Rock: Black Resistance in a Revolutionary Age*. Princeton, NJ: Princeton University Press, 1991.

Fuentes, Marisa J., and Deborah Gray White, eds. *Scarlet and Black: Slavery and Dispossession in Rutgers History*. Vol. 1. New Brunswick, NJ: Rutgers University Press, 2016.

Geffken, Rick, and Don Burden. *The Story of Shrewsbury, Revisited 1965–2015.* Shrewsbury, NJ: Shrewsbury Historical Society, 2015.

Geffken, Rick, and Muriel J. Smith. *Hidden History of Monmouth County.* Charleston, SC: The History Press, 2019.

Gigantino, James J., II. *The Ragged Road to Abolition: Slavery and Freedom in New Jersey, 1775–1865.* Philadelphia: University of Pennsylvania Press, 2015.

———. "Trading in Jersey Souls: New Jersey and the Interstate Slave Trade." *Pennsylvania History: A Journal of Mid-Atlantic Studies* 77, no. 3 (Summer 2010): 281–302.

Gordon, Robert Boyd. *American Iron, 1607–1900.* Baltimore, MD: Johns Hopkins University Press, 1996.

Gordon, Thomas F. *A Gazetteer of the State of New Jersey.* Trenton, NJ: Daniel Fenton, 1834.

Grabas, Joseph A. *Owning New Jersey: Historic Tales of War, Property Disputes & the Pursuit of Happiness.* Charleston, SC: The History Press, 2014.

Gragg, Larry Dale. *The Quaker Community on Barbados: Challenging the Culture of the Planter Class.* Columbia: University of Missouri Press, 2009.

Greason, Walter D., PhD. *The Path to Freedom: Black Families in New Jersey.* Charleston, SC: The History Press, 2010.

Green, Howard L., ed. *Words That Make New Jersey History: A Primary Source Reader.* New Brunswick, NJ: Rutgers University Press, 1995.

Greene, Larry A. "A History of Afro-Americans in New Jersey." *Journal of the Rutgers University Libraries* 56 (1994): 4–71.

Grimsted, David. *American Mobbing, 1828–1861: Toward Civil War.* New York: Oxford University Press, 1998.

Gronniosaw, James Albert Ukawsaw. *A Narrative of the Most Remarkable Particulars in the Life of James Albert Ukawsaw Gronniosaw, an African Prince, as Related by Himself.* Bath, UK: W. Gye, 1772.

Hack, Timothy. "Janus-Faced: Post-Revolutionary Slavery in East and West Jersey, 1784–1804." *New Jersey History Studies in State and Regional History* 127, no. 1 (2012): 1–36. https://njh.libraries.rutgers.edu.

Hageman, John Frelinghuysen. *History of Princeton and Its Institutions.* Vol. 1. Philadelphia: J.B. Lippincott & Co., 1879.

Harris, Peter. *Income Tax in Common Law Jurisdictions: From the Origins to 1820.* New York: Cambridge University Press, 2006.

Harvey, Cornelius Burnham, ed. *Genealogical History of Hudson and Bergen Counties, New Jersey.* New York: New Jersey Genealogical Publishing Company, 1900.

Hearn, Daniel Allen. *Legal Executions in New Jersey: A Comprehensive Registry, 1691–1963*. Jefferson, NC: McFarland & Co., 2005.

Heckscher, Morrison H., and Leslie Greene Bowman. *American Rococo, 1750–1775: Elegance in Ornament*. New York: Harry N. Abrams, 1992.

Hennelly, Bob. "History Is Alive but We Have to Have the Courage to Keep Looking for It." *InsiderNJ*, July 3, 2018. https://www.insidernj.com.

Heston, Alfred M., ed. *South Jersey: A History, 1664–1924*. New York: Lewis Historical Publishing Co., 1924.

Historical Society of Pennsylvania. William Trent (d. 1724) Ledger. https://hsp.org.

Hodges, Graham Russell Gao. *Black New Jersey, 1664 to the Present Day*. New Brunswick, NJ: Rutgers University Press, 2019.

———. *Root & Branch: African Americans in New York & East Jersey*. Chapel Hill: University of North Carolina Press, 1999.

———. *Slavery and Freedom in the Rural North: African Americans in Monmouth County, New Jersey, 1665–1865*. Lanham, MD: Rowman & Littlefield Publishers, 1997.

Hodges, Graham Russell Gao, and Alan Edward Brown, eds. *"Pretends to Be Free": Runaway Slave Advertisements from Colonial and Revolutionary New York and New Jersey*. New York: Garland Publishing, 1994.

Hodges, Graham Russell Gao, Susan Hawkes Cook and Alan Edward Brown. *The Black Loyalist Directory: African Americans in Exile After the American Revolution*. New York: Garland Publishing/New England Historic Genealogical Society, 1996.

Holmes, Isaac. *An Account of the United States of America: Derived from Actual Observation*. London: Caxton Press, 1823.

Honeyman, A. Van Duren, ed. "The Revolutionary War Record of Samuel Sutphin, Slave." *Somerset County Historical Quarterly* 3 (July 1914): 186–90.

Horne, Gerald. *The Counter-Revolution of 1776: Slave Resistance and the Origins of the United States of America*. New York: New York University Press, 2014.

Hornor, William S. *This Old Monmouth of Ours*. Freehold, NJ: Moreau Bros., 1932.

Hugh, Howard. *Houses of the Founding Fathers: The Men Who Made America and the Way They Lived*. New York: Artisan, 2007.

Hutchinson, Richard S. *Monmouth County New Jersey Deeds, Books A, B, C, & D*. Bowie, MD: Heritage Books, 2000.

Innis, Lolita Buckner. "James Collins Johnson: The Princeton Fugitive Slave." *Princeton & Slavery Project*. https://slavery.princeton.edu.

Irwin, Richard T. *Asserting Title to Liberty: New Jersey, Slavery, the Underground Railroad; A Path to Emancipation*. Madison: Historiographers of New Jersey, 2018.

Jackson, Maurice, and Susan Kozel, eds. *Quakers and Their Allies in the Abolitionist Cause, 1754–1808*. New York: Routledge, 2015.

Jelliffe, Thelma K. *Achter Coll to Zoning, Historical Notes on Middletown, N.J.* Middletown, NJ: Academy Press, 1982.

Kaplan, Sidney, and Emma Nogrady Kaplan. *The Black Presence in the Era of the American Revolution*. Amherst: University of Massachusetts Press, 1989.

Keith, George. *Account Book, 1685–1699*. Freehold, New Jersey Collection, Monmouth County Historical Association Museum.

Kidd, Sue Monk. *The Invention of Wings*. New York: Penguin Books, 2014.

Klein, Herbert S. *The Middle Passage: Comparative Studies in the Atlantic Slave Trade*. Princeton, NJ: Princeton University Press, 1978.

Krasner, Barbara, and the Kearny Museum. *Images of America Kearny*. Charleston, SC: Arcadia Publishing, 2000.

Kull, Irving S., ed. *New Jersey: A History*. New York: American Historical Society, 1930.

Langford, Kristal C. Lost Souls Public Memorial Project. https://lostsoulsmemorialnj.org.

Larison, C.W., MD. *Silvia DuBois (Now 116 Yers Old), A Biografy of the Slav Who Whipt Her Mistres and Ganed Her Fredom*. Ringos, NJ: C.W. Larison Publisher, 1883.

Lee, Francis Bazley, ed. *History of Trenton, New Jersey: The Record of Its Early Settlement and Corporate Progress*. Trenton, NJ: F.T. Smiley & Co., 1895.

Lewis Historical Publications. *History of Monmouth County, New Jersey, 1664–1920*. New York: Lewis Historical Publications, 1922.

Linn, William Alexander. "Slavery in Bergen County, N.J." *Papers and Proceedings of the Bergen County Historical Society* no. 1 (1905).

Lundy, Benjamin. *The Poetical Works of Elizabeth Margaret Chandler with a Memoir of Her Life and Character*. Philadelphia: Lemuel Howell, 1836.

Lurie, Maxine N., ed. *A New Jersey Anthology*. New Brunswick, NJ: Rutgers University Press, 1994.

Lurie, Maxine N., and Marc Mappen. *The Encyclopedia of New Jersey*. New Brunswick, NJ: Rutgers University Press, 2004.

Lurie, Maxine N., and Richard Veit. *New Jersey: A History of the Garden State*. New Brunswick, NJ: Rutgers University Press, 2012.

MacLean, Alexander. *The Underground Railroad in Hudson County*. Papers read before the Historical Society of Hudson County, 1908.

Magness, Phillip W., and Sebastian N. Page. *Colonization after Emancipation: Lincoln and the Movement for Black Resettlement.* Columbia: University of Missouri Press, 2011.

Malone, Ann Patton. *Sweet Chariot: Slave Family and Household Structure in Nineteenth-Century Louisiana.* Chapel Hill: University of North Carolina Press, 1992.

Mandeville, Ernest W. *The Story of Middletown: The Oldest Settlement in New Jersey.* Middletown, NJ: Christ Church, 1927.

Marrin, Richard B. *Runaways of Colonial New Jersey: Indentured Servants, Slaves, Deserters, and Prisoners, 1720–1781.* Westminster, MD: Heritage Books, 2007.

Marshall, Kenneth Edward. *Manhood Enslaved: Bondmen in Eighteenth- and Early Nineteenth-Century New Jersey.* Rochester, NY: Rochester University Press, 2011.

Martin, Alvia Disbrow. *At the Headwaters of Cheesequake Creek.* Madison Township, NJ: Madison Township Historical Society, 1979.

McConville, Brendan. *These Daring Disturbers of the Public Peace: The Struggle for Property and Power in Early New Jersey.* Ithaca, NY: Cornell University Press, 1999.

McCormick, Richard Patrick. *New Jersey from Colony to State, 1609–1789.* Princeton, NJ: D. Van Nostrand Company, 1964.

McIntosh, Tabitha. "White Rascals in New Jersey: A Representative Anecdote." Unpublished personal correspondence with author.

Meacham, Jon. *Thomas Jefferson: The Art of Power.* New York: Random House, 2012.

Mellick, Andrew D. *The Story of an Old Farm; Or, Life in New Jersey in the Eighteenth Century.* Somerville, NJ: *Unionist-Gazette*, 1889.

Michals, Debra, ed. "Harriet Tubman, ca. 1820–1913." National Women's History Museum. 2015. https://www.womenshistory.org.

Miller, John Chester. *The Wolf by the Ears: Thomas Jefferson and Slavery.* New York: Free Press, 1977.

Mills, Weymer Jay. *Historic Houses of New Jersey.* Philadelphia: J.B. Lippincott & Co., 1902.

Mitnick, Barbara J., ed. *New Jersey in the American Revolution.* New Brunswick, NJ: Rivergate Books, 2005.

Mitros, David. *Jacob Green and the Slavery Debate in Revolutionary Morris County, New Jersey.* Morristown, NJ: Morris County Heritage Commission, 1993.

———, ed. *Slave Records of Morris County, New Jersey: 1756–1841.* Morristown, NJ: Morris County Heritage Commission, 1991.

Monmouth County Genealogy Society. *Middletown Town Book Two, 1699–1848*. Lincroft, NJ: Monmouth County Genealogy Society, 2014. Reprint of original.

Monmouth Democrat (Freehold, NJ), various dates.

Moss, Simeon F. "The Persistence of Slavery and Involuntary Servitude in a Free State (1685–1866)." *Journal of Negro History* 35, no. 3 (July 1950): 289–314.

Mr. Local History Project. "A Unique Bedminster Cemetery—'God's Acre.'" http://www.mrlocalhistory.org.

Muller, F.L. "Cooper of the Northern New Jersey Piedmont." *Unearthing New Jersey* 6, no. 1 (Winter 2010).

Murphy, Andrew R. *William Penn: A Life*. New York: Oxford University Press, 2019.

Nelson, William, ed. *Documents Relating to the Colonial History of the State of New Jersey*. Paterson, NJ: Press Printing and Publishing, 1899.

———. *History of the City of Paterson and the County of Passaic, New Jersey*. Paterson, NJ: Press Printing and Publishing, 1901.

———. *New Jersey Archives, Extracts from American Newspapers, Relating to New Jersey, 1704–1775*. Paterson, NJ: Call Printing and Publishing, 1902.

———. *New Jersey Biographical and Genealogical Notes*. Newark: New Jersey Historical Society, 1916.

New Jersey Historical Society. *The Papers of Lewis Morris, Governor of the Province of New Jersey from 1738 to 1746*. Freeport, NY: Books for Library Press, 1970. Reprint of 1852 original.

New York Times, various dates.

Nickalls, John L., ed. *The Journal of George Fox*. Cambridge, UK: Cambridge University Press, 1952.

Oberg, Barbara B. *Women in the American Revolution: Gender, Politics, and the Domestic World*. Charlottesville: University of Virginia Press, 2019.

Parris, Frederic J. *The Case of the Rev. Samuel Cooke: Loyalist*. Freehold, NJ: Monmouth County Historical Association, 1975.

Pickard, Kate E.R. *The Kidnapped and the Ransomed*. Syracuse, NY: William T. Hamilton, 1856.

Pickersgill, Harold E., and John Patrick Wall, eds. *History of Middlesex County, New Jersey, 1664–1920*. Vol. 1. New York: Lewis Historical Publishing, 1921.

Pitney, Henry Cooper. *A History of Morris County, New Jersey: Embracing Upwards of Two Centuries, 1710–1913*. New York: Lewis Historical Publications, 1914.

Pomfret, John E. *Province of East New Jersey, 1609–1702: Princeton History of New Jersey, 1609–1702. The Rebellious Proprietary.* Princeton, NJ: Princeton University Press, 1962.

Postma, Johannes. *The Dutch in the Atlantic Slave Trade, 1600–1815.* New York: Cambridge University Press, 1990.

Prowell, George Reeser. *The History of Camden County, New Jersey.* Philadelphia: L.J. Richards & Co., 1886.

Raser, Edward J. *New Jersey Graveyard & Gravestone Inscriptions Locators: Monmouth County.* New Brunswick: Genealogical Society of New Jersey Monmouth County, 2002.

Raum, John O. *The History of New Jersey: From Its Earliest Settlement to the Present Time, Including a Brief Historical Account of the First Discoveries and Settlement of the Country.* Philadelphia: John E. Potter and Co., 1877.

Rizzo, Dennis. *Parallel Communities: The Underground Railroad in South Jersey.* Charleston, SC: The History Press, 2008.

Rossignol, Marie-Jeanne, and Bertrand Van Ruymbeke, eds. *The Atlantic World of Anthony Benezet (1713–1784): From French Reformation to North American Antislavery Activism.* Leiden, Netherlands: Koninklijke Brill, 2017.

Salter, Edwin. *A History of Monmouth and Ocean Counties.* Bayonne, NJ: E. Gardner & Son, 1890.

Salter, Edwin, and George C. Beekman. *Old Times in Old Monmouth.* Freehold, NJ: *Monmouth Democrat,* 1874.

Schama, Simon. *Rough Crossings, Britain, the Slaves and the American Revolution.* New York: HarperCollins, 2005.

Scott, W.R. *The Constitution and Finance of the Royal African Company of England from Its Foundation till 1720.* N.p.: American Historical Review, 1903.

Sheridan, Eugene R. *Lewis Morris 1671–1746: A Study in Early American Politics.* Syracuse, NY: Syracuse University Press, 1981.

Shomo, Robert E. "Cedar View Cemetery, Original Land/Lot Owners, A History of People, A Record of Yesterday." Personal correspondence.

Shorto, Russell. *The Island at the Center of the World: The Epic Story of Dutch Manhattan and the Forgotten Colony That Shaped America.* New York: Doubleday, 2004.

Shourds, Thomas. *History and Genealogy of Fenwick's Colony.* Bridgetown, NJ: George F. Nixon, 1876.

Sickler, Joseph Sheppard. *The History of Salem County, New Jersey.* Salem, NJ: Sunbeam Publishing, 1937.

Siebert, Wilbur Henry. *The Underground Railroad from Slavery to Freedom.* New York: Macmillan, 1898.

Simpson, Jack, and Matt Rutherford. *A Bibliography of African American Family History at the Newberry Library.* Chicago: Newberry Library, 2005.

Singer, Alan J. *New York and Slavery: Time to Teach the Truth.* Albany: State University of New York Press, 2008.

Slave Manumissions, 1787–1844 and Slave Births, 1804–1848. Monmouth County Archives (division of Monmouth County Clerk's Office). Manalapan, New Jersey.

Slesinski, Jason J. *Along the Raritan River: South Amboy to New Brunswick.* Charleston, SC: Arcadia Publishing, 2014.

Smith, Samuel. *The History of the Colony of Nova Caesaria, or New Jersey.* Philadelphia: James Parker, 1765.

Smith, Samuel Stelle. *Lewis Morris, Anglo-American Statesman ca.1613–1691.* Atlantic Highlands, NJ: Humanities Press, 1983.

Snell, James P., and Franklin Ellis, comps. *History of Hunterdon and Somerset Counties, New Jersey.* Philadelphia: Everts & Peck, 1881.

Soderlund, Jean R. *Quakers and Slavery: A Divided Spirit.* Princeton, NJ: Princeton University Press, 1985.

Stein, R. Conrad, and Charlotte Taylor. *The Underground Railroad.* New York: Enslow Publishing, 2016.

Still, James. *Early Recollections and Life of Dr. James Still.* N.p.: J.B. Lippincott & Co., 1877.

Still, William. *The Underground Railroad: A Record of Facts, Authentic Narratives, Letters, Etc.* Philadelphia: Porter & Coates, 1872.

Stillwell, John E., ed. *Unrecorded Wills and Inventories, Monmouth County, NJ.* New Orleans, LA: Polyanthos Press, 1975.

Stockton, Frank R. *Stories of New Jersey.* New York, NJ: American Book Company, 1896.

Strassburger, John Robert. "The Origins and Establishment of the Morris Family in the Society and Politics of New York and New Jersey, 1630–1746." PhD thesis, Princeton University, 1976.

Streets, David H. *Slave Genealogy: A Research Guide with Case Studies.* Bowie, MD: Heritage Books, 1986.

Stuart, Andrea. *Sugar in the Blood.* New York: Vintage Books, 2012.

Temple, Brian. *Philadelphia Quakers and the Antislavery Movement.* Jefferson, NC: McFarland, 1955.

Thomas, Hugh. *The Slave Trade: The Story of the Atlantic Slave Trade: 1440–1870.* New York: Simon and Schuster, 1997.

Tomek, Beverly C. "Fugitives from Slavery." Encyclopedia of Greater Philadelphia. 2016. https://philadelphiaencyclopedia.org.

Toop, Marion. *Iron Kettles, Home Brew and Epitaphs: A History of Lincroft.* Lincroft, NJ: privately printed, 1980.

Toplin, Robert Brent. "Peter Still Versus the Peculiar Institution." *Kent State University Press* 13, no. 4 (December 1967): 340–49. https://muse.jhu.edu.

Trust Company of New Jersey. *History of Hudson County and the Old Village of Bergen.* New York: Bartlett Orr Press, 1921.

Van Winkle, Daniel. *History of the Municipalities of Hudson County, New Jersey, 1630–1923.* Vol. 1. New York: Lewis Historical Publishing, 1924.

Walker, Edwin Robert. "A History of Trenton, 1679–1929. Two Hundred and Fifty Years of a Notable Town with Links in Four Centuries." http://www.trentonhistory.org.

Walling, Richard S. *Men of Color at the Battle of Monmouth, June 28, 1778: The Role of African Americans and Native Americans at Monmouth.* Hightstown, NJ: Longstreet House, 1994.

Watson, John F. *Annals of Philadelphia and Pennsylvania, in the Olden Time.* Philadelphia: Edwin S. Stuart, 1884.

Wax, Darold D. "Quaker Merchants and the Slave Trade in Colonial Pennsylvania." *Pennsylvania Magazine of History and Biography* 86, no. 2 (April 1962): 143–59. https://www.jstor.org.

Weeks, Daniel J. *Not for Filthy Lucre's Sake: Richard Saltar and the Antiproprietary Movement in East New Jersey, 1665–1707.* Bethlehem, PA: Lehigh University Press, 2001.

Weeks, Lyman Horace. *Prominent Families of New York.* New York: Historical Co., 1898.

Whitcomb, Royden Page. *First History of Bayonne, New Jersey.* Bayonne, NJ: R.P. Whitcomb, 1904.

Whitehead, Russell F., and Frank Chouteau Brown, eds. *Early Homes of New York and the Mid-Atlantic States.* New York: Arno Press, 1977.

Whitehead, William A., ed. *Documents Relating to the Colonial History of the State of New Jersey.* Vol. II, 1687–1703. Newark, NJ: *Daily Advertiser* Printing House, 1881.

———. *The Papers of Lewis Morris, Governor of the Province of New Jersey from 1738–1746.* New York: George P. Putnam, 1852.

Wildes, Harry Emerson. *William Penn: A Biography.* New York: Macmillan, 1974.

Williams, Oscar R. *African Americans and Colonial Legislation in the Middle Colonies.* New York: Taylor & Francis, 1998.

Williams, Seymour. *The Rogers House, Near Springside, Burlington County, New Jersey.* Rahway, NJ: Historic American Buildings Survey, 1937.

Winfield, Charles Hardenburg. *History of the County of Hudson, New Jersey: From Its Earliest Settlement to the Present Time.* New York: Kennard & Hay, 1874.

———. *History of the Land Titles in Hudson County, N.J., 1609–1871.* New York: Wynkoop and Hallenbeck, 1872.

Winter, John, D. *The Civil War in Louisiana.* Baton Rouge: Louisiana State University Press, 1963.

Wolgemuth, Kathleen L. "Woodrow Wilson and Federal Segregation." *Journal of Negro History* 44, no. 2 (April 1959): 158–73. https://www.jstor.org.

Woodward, Carl Raymond. *Ploughs and Politicks: Charles Read of New Jersey and His Notes on Agriculture, 1715–1774.* New Brunswick, NJ: Rutgers University Press, 1941.

Woodward, E.M., and John F. Hageman. *History of Burlington and Mercer Counties, New Jersey: With Biographical Sketches of Many of Their Pioneers and Prominent Men.* N.p.: J.B. Lippincott & Co., 1883.

Woodward, Herbert P. *Copper Mines and Mining in New Jersey.* Trenton: New Jersey Geological Survey, 1944.

Woolman, John. *Considerations on the Keeping of Negroes.* Philadelphia: B. Franklin and D. Hall, 1762.

———. *The Journal and Essays of John Woolman.* New York: Macmillan, 1922.

Work Projects Administration. *Bergen County Panorama.* Hackensack, NJ: Bergen County Board of Chosen Freeholders, 1941.

Wright, Giles R. *Afro-Americans in New Jersey: A Short History.* Trenton: New Jersey Historical Commission, Department of State, 1988.

———. "Moving Toward Breaking the Chains: Black New Jerseyans and the American Revolution." In *New Jersey in the American Revolution.* New Brunswick, NJ: Rivergate Books, 2005.

Wright, Marion Thompson. "A Period of Transition, 1804–1865." *Journal of Negro History* 28, no. 2 (April 1943): 176–89.

———. "The Quakers as Social Workers Among Negros in New Jersey from 1763 to 1804." *Bulletin of Friends Historical Association* 30, no. 2 (Autumn 1941): 79–88. https://www.jstor.org.

Yamin, Rebecca. *Rediscovering Raritan Landing: An Adventure in New Jersey Archaeology.* Trenton: New Jersey Department of Transportation, 2011.

Yannielli, Joseph. "Princeton's Fugitive Slaves." *Princeton & Slavery.* https://slavery.princeton.edu.

Zook, George Frederick. *The Company of Royal Adventurers Trading into Africa.* Lancaster, PA: New Era Printing Company, 1919.

INDEX

ABOUT THE AUTHOR

*Office of the Monmouth
County Clerk.*

Rick Geffken has written numerous articles on various aspects of New Jersey history for local newspapers, magazines and newsletters. An energetic and popular speaker, he has spoken at the New Jersey History & Historic Preservation symposia, Rutgers and Monmouth Universities and dozens of libraries and historical societies throughout the Garden State and has appeared on the New Jersey cable television show *Family Historian.*

Besides presenting talks about his published books, Rick has spoken about "Simon Lake and John Holland, New Jersey's Submarine Inventors"; "Amazing New Jersey, People and Places of the Garden State"; and "The Morrises: New Jersey Founding Family."

Rick is a trustee of the Shrewsbury Historical Society, past president and a trustee of the Jersey Coast Heritage Museum at Sandlass House, former publisher of the *Monmouth Connection* and a member of the Navesink Maritime Historical Association and the Monmouth County Historical Association. He is currently heading up a project called the New Jersey Slavery Records Index.

Rick's publications include *The Story of Shrewsbury Revisited, 1965–2015*; *Lost Amusement Parks of the North Jersey Shore* (Arcadia Publishing); *Highland*

Beach, Gateway to the Jersey Shore, 1888–1962; *Hidden History of Monmouth County* (The History Press); and *To Preserve and Protect: Profiles of People Who Recorded the History and Heritage of Monmouth County, New Jersey*.

Rick has owned and operated several small businesses, taught secondary school mathematics, was an adjunct professor at Ocean County Community and enjoyed a successful career with Hewlett-Packard. A retired U.S. Army officer and decorated Vietnam veteran, he holds a bachelor of science in economics from St. Peter's University, a secondary teaching certificate from Monmouth University and a master of arts in social science from Montclair State University.

For information about speaking engagements, email Rickg0817@yahoo.com.